FÉLIX GUATTARI AND THE ANCIENTS

Also Available from Bloomsbury

Deleuze and Guattari, Kenneth J. Surin
Ecosophical Aesthetics, Patricia MacCormack and Colin Gardner

FÉLIX GUATTARI AND THE ANCIENTS

Theatrical Dialogues in Early Philosophy

GARY GENOSKO AND CARLOS A. SEGOVIA

BLOOMSBURY ACADEMIC
LONDON • NEW YORK • OXFORD • NEW DELHI • SYDNEY

BLOOMSBURY ACADEMIC
Bloomsbury Publishing Plc, 50 Bedford Square, London, WC1B 3DP, UK
Bloomsbury Publishing Inc, 1385 Broadway, New York, NY 10018, USA
Bloomsbury Publishing Ireland, 29 Earlsfort Terrace, Dublin 2, D02 AY28, Ireland

BLOOMSBURY, BLOOMSBURY ACADEMIC and the Diana logo are trademarks of Bloomsbury Publishing Plc

First published in Great Britain 2025

Copyright © Gary Genosko and Carlos A. Segovia, and Contributors, 2025

Gary Genosko and Carlos A. Segovia, have asserted their right under the Copyright, Designs and Patents Act, 1988, to be identified as Editors of this work.

For legal purposes the Acknowledgments on p. xxiii constitute an extension of this copyright page.

Cover design: Ben Anslow
Cover image: Bust of Parmenides (Elea, 515 BC-450 BC), pre-Socratic Greek philosopher. Marble statue, from Velia, Campania, Italy. (Photo by DE AGOSTINI PICTURE LIBRARY / Getty Images)

All rights reserved. No part of this publication may be: i) reproduced or transmitted in any form, electronic or mechanical, including photocopying, recording or by means of any information storage or retrieval system without prior permission in writing from the publishers; or ii) used or reproduced in any way for the training, development or operation of artificial intelligence (AI) technologies, including generative AI technologies. The rights holders expressly reserve this publication from the text and data mining exception as per Article 4(3) of the Digital Single Market Directive (EU) 2019/790.

Bloomsbury Publishing Plc does not have any control over, or responsibility for, any third-party websites referred to or in this book. All internet addresses given in this book were correct at the time of going to press. The author and publisher regret any inconvenience caused if addresses have changed or sites have ceased to exist, but can accept no responsibility for any such changes.

A catalogue record for this book is available from the British Library.

A catalog record for this book is available from the Library of Congress.

ISBN:	HB:	978-1-3504-6889-4
	PB:	978-1-3504-6888-7
	ePDF:	978-1-3504-6890-0
	eBook:	978-1-3504-6891-7

Typeset by Integra Software Services Pvt. Ltd.
Printed and bound in Great Britain

To find out more about our authors and books visit www.bloomsbury.com and sign up for our newsletters.

CONTENTS

Foreword: Félix Guattari's Theatrical Dialogues and the Return to Early Philosophy vii
Gary Genosko and Carlos A. Segovia
Acknowledgments xxiii

PART ONE Source Materials and Translations of *Parmenides* 1

0   Félix Guattari, *Parménide*, Facsimile Edition 3
1   French Transcribed by Stéphane Nadaud 19
2   English Translated by Gary Genosko 25
3   Spanish Translated by Carlos A. Segovia 31
4   Japanese Translated by Mahoro Murasawa 39
5   German Translated by Iloe Ariss 45
6   Polish Translated by Benjamin Bandosz 51
7   Russian Translated by Mikhail Fedorchenko 57

PART TWO Commentaries 63

8   From Logic to Rhythm 65
    Gary Genosko
9   Being, Oneness and Desire in Guattari's *Parménide* 79
    Carlos A. Segovia

10 Guattari's Constructivism and the Theater Machine of Revolution 95
    Mahoro Murasawa

11 The Trouble with People and Things 107
    Iloe Ariss

12 Infernal Machines: The Guattaro-Witkacian Theatre of Theory 119
    Benjamin Bandosz

PART THREE Reference Texts 131

13 Portrait of Félix Guattari as a Playwright 133
    Flore Garcin-Marrou, Translated by Jay Hetrick

14 Socrates 149
    Félix Guattari Translated by Solène Nicolas, Arranged by Flore Garcin-Marrou

Contributors 166
Index 168

FOREWORD: *FÉLIX GUATTARI'S THEATRICAL DIALOGUES AND THE RETURN TO EARLY PHILOSOPHY*

Gary Genosko and Carlos A. Segovia

Heretofore unpublished, like the majority of his theatrical dialogs, Félix Guattari's *Parménide/Parmenides* is a brief but extremely suggestive dialog—in fact, an ontological drama—in which Guattari's concerns with the early history of Western philosophy, including Plato and the pre-Socratics, overlap with contemporary theater and performance. Paired with *Socrates*, the only theatrical piece that Guattari wrote to have been performed, *Parmenides* is introduced here in this small volume with the facsimile edition of the original manuscript, handwritten on fourteen pages in quarto of circa thirteen lines each, on notepaper in a distinctive handwriting. The transcription of the French, prepared by Stéphane Nadaud, is followed by annotated translations in English (Gary Genosko), Spanish (Carlos Segovia), German (Iloe Ariss), Japanese (Mahoro Murasawa), Polish (Ben Bandosz), and Russian (Mikhail Fedorchenko). These are followed by extended commentaries from our international translation team, including the editors. The book concludes with documents and studies—an updated existing English translation of *Socrates*, and Flore

Garcin-Marrou's reflections on Guattari's activity as a playwright based on her archival work.

How did Guattari find Parmenides? Certainly, he found inspiration in the figures of ancient Greek thought as well as in the early metaphysics and styles of reasoning developed by them. There are preferred routes: through Plato's dialogs,[1] and in edited collections in French. Guattari relied on Jean Voilquin's edited and translated collection, *Les Penseurs grecs avant Socrate. De Thalès de Milet à Prodicos*,[2] for his insights into Parmenides and others. This is the volume he cites in *Schizoanalytic Cartographies*,[3] in the section on time where he attempts to define Parmenidean time as "unary"[4]; at this extreme the singular component is that it is an unchanging, timeless time, describable as anti-Heraclitean, and opposed to becoming—yet coextensive with pure immanence.[5] Since time for Guattari is composite and temporal components may be combined, even the other extreme of computer-aided time analysis of some phenomenon in real-time could come into contact with the atemporality of reality, in an imagined scenario, through intermediate temporal components.[6]

However, Guattari's purpose is to actually displace time and its attachment to Being in favor of enunciation, which is given "precedence" over the two Heideggerian key concepts, thus marking a displacement, but also a recognition of the import of an ontology sensitive to chaosmosis, rather than fundamental in the Heideggerian sense.[7] Guattari, anyway, was not predisposed to view Parmenides, who is commonly taken to be the first philosopher to think Being in a fundamental way, in terms of Voilquin's approach, which emphasized colorlessness: "Parmenides remains, not without reason, the master of the cold and inexpressive concept of Being."[8] As we will see, one cannot describe Guattari's dialog *Parmenides* as lacking color and soul! However, Guattari quotes from Voilquin's selection from Parmenides' proem "On Nature," titled "La voie et la vérité," regarding the support (in fact, the reciprocal presupposition) between thinking and Being that is there to be known: "the act of thinking and the object of thought are indistinguishable. Without Being, in which it is uttered, the act of thinking could not be located."[9] The "being of enunciation" or expression (not necessarily discursive) is for Guattari, to contrast with Heidegger who takes an etymological route (i.e., who makes of Being the elusive object of an aporetic meta-enunciative and meta-discursive enquiry), a thinking that depends on Being in order to be expressed. There is no thought without Being, yet for Heidegger we are not yet thinking Being in the correct manner.[10]

What does Guattari want from this? He pursues in the *Cartographies* the "fractalization" of enunciation, extending the unary or univocal time into a "Parmenidean immanence" that reflects the unity of thought and object of thought, what Hanjo Berressem astutely describes as an "ecological adequation between the world and its entities"[11]: or, for Guattari, "neither inside nor outside, neither figure nor ground, it is a pure body without organs, a pure self-referential affirmation."[12] What Guattari wants from Parmenides in his ontology is a pole that he can contrast with a non-unary, less undifferentiated, field and then moderate the interactions between them (as the two disjunctive dimensions, as it were, of what, from 1971 onward, he calls a single "plane of consistency") in the forms of diagrams.[13] This, then, is a philosophical recipe for interaction that lends itself to the form of a theatrical dialog. This is the core of the theatrical dialog, in which the difficulties of maintaining a univocal claim that Being is-there and does not require any extra articulations are exposed. The source material includes Parmenidean thought in the surviving fragments and proem, and the appearance of the figure of Parmenides in Plato's dialog *Parmenides*, in which a young Socrates meets a seasoned, senior thinker in an intergenerational confrontation for the ages. Aristotle's critique of Parmenidean univocity in the name of change, becoming and plurivocity, in the *Physics* and *Metaphysics*, as wandering astray from physics to metaphysics, would draw a short circle.[14] But these materials do not confine Guattari. On the contrary, they open up the possibilities for investigating the sinuosities of thought, action, and character, and the fragility of logic is at least at par with the pacing of the script. We can appreciate these facets in a fully realized play such as *Socrates* where the couple meets a philosophical friend, Challenger, the professor of Rhizomatics, borrowed from Arthur Conan Doyle, and inserted into the "Geology of Morals" plateau[15]; and, in reverse Kafkaesque fashion, he comes through the ceiling and stretches downward, rather than a bent-to-straightened opening of a head that pushes through the ceiling upon extending itself, one of the features of Kafka's story writing analyzed in the jointly authored *Kafka* book.[16]

A nonphilosophical or, rather, anti-philosophical source for Guattari's interest in Parmenides is Jacques Lacan, his analyst. Staying with Parmenides, if only for the sake of fiction, rubs up against Lacan's statements in *Encore* to the effect that "I distinguish myself from the language of being." For the language that Lacan spoke was about "what there isn't."[17] Thus, the Parmenidean One was split, the subject and world torn asunder, fullness drained through dehiscence. Lacan made it evident that "the fact that being is presumed to think— is what founds the philosophical tradition starting from Parmenides.

Parmenides was wrong and Heraclitus was right."[18] Breaking from the tradition, which begins with Parmenides, alerts us to the need to return to Parmenides before one returns to Plato. Yet it was the poetry of Parmenides that captured and held Lacan's interest. This is the decisive point. Lacan wrote: "Fortunately, Parmenides actually wrote poems. ... It is precisely because he was a poet that Parmenides says what he has to say to us in the least stupid of manners. Otherwise, the idea that being is and non-being is not, I don't know what that means to you, but personally I find that stupid."[19] The poems are valuable for Lacan because they are in the spirit of his interpreters, "secret sources" for understanding his thought, in their innocence and for what they prefigure: a severity more terrible, mathematization, if we are to believe Alain Badiou's discovery of a "paradoxical inversion" in which "poetry was the closest thing to mathematization available to the pre-Socratics. Poetic form is the innocence of the grandiose."[20] Stupidity is graced with traces of a promising innocence. As a playwright, however, Guattari found the early figures of philosophy fertile ground for exploration of the themes of attachment to the single, grand idea, a kind of madness exudes from statements about the One, and equally strong responses to it by those who witness such possession and take positions with or against it—a Heraclitean line of flight; a Zenonian provocation about in the inadequacies of plurality. This is an ancient preoccupation to be sure that Guattari brings to life, that he undoubtedly lived through in his relationship with Lacan.[21]

Yet Deleuze's ontological univocism lurks, too, behind Guattari's problematization and creative rewriting of Parmenides' unary temporality in the *Cartographies*, which indirectly allows Guattari to take a stand vis-à-vis Deleuze's philosophy that re-signifies the value of the multiple, while admitting that the idea of unity can and should serve as a referential pole for it[22]—an issue that *Parménide/Parmenides* explores in a beautifully playful way.

A few remarks on the organization of this volume are in order.

The Guattarian prospect of producing new axes of reference that undermine older, tired binaries inspired us to initiate a project in which we first followed connections between a modern French psychoanalyst with a penchant for writing dramaturgy, and two ancient philosophical figures that inspired him, Parmenides and Socrates. However, secondly, we put into play a process that would generate multiple translations of the original French theatrical dialog, hitherto unpublished and untranslated—English, Spanish, German, Japanese, Polish, and Russian—with the goal of producing a multilingual edition that overcame the standard of a single language-to-language translation project and, instead, traversed diverse linguistic planes.

In doing so we wanted to acknowledge the internationalism of Guattari studies, in a spirit that we hoped would loosen meaningful elements that might otherwise remain dormant, to productively transform the text. So, to this end, we introduced a series of "ands" between Guattari's *Parménide* and the aforementioned languages of translation. "And" is less a bridge, or a crossroads between two, and more of a series of contact points of mutual entanglement. We hope that our readers will continue the process of mutual imbrication among the original and its translations and among the translations themselves. A multilingual edition is designed to become transversal and to encourage creative reworkings. With only one exception, the translators have contributed interpretive essays responding to the source text, in order to reverse any lingering sense of self-effacement that might be implied by producing a translation in the first place. Our translators are visible, beyond whatever paratextual traces they may have left in their renditions, and beyond the standard of a translator's introduction. Their fluencies have expanded into both cultural and disciplinary spaces of interest and to existing aesthetic themes of importance in Guattari's work. This can be seen most clearly in the contribution of Japanese translator Mahoro Murasawa, who pursues the connection between Guattari and Butoh dancer Min Tanaka; and the Polish translator Ben Bandosz pursues Guattari's connection to the theater of Witkacy—Stanislav Witkiewicz—through the intersecting lines of language and culture. In some instances, these lines cross and then turn back; thus, Gary Genosko's English version is developed with reference to modern French philosophy and its ancient ontological preoccupations; whereas, Carlos Segovia's Spanish translation gives rise to the problems of ontology through a neglected figure in Guattari studies, German philosopher Gottfried Wilhelm Leibniz; thus, a barely visible line is excavated. In her German translation, Iloe Ariss uses Heidegger's essay "Das Ding" to expose the conundrum of the one and many as it unfolds in the play toward a ribald end. Several commentaries enlist phenomenology as a key reference to excavate Guattari's theater of ideas. Perhaps, then, the presentation of the *Parmenides* dialog can contribute to a more nuanced understanding of the role that phenomenology plays in Guattari's thinking. Although the difference between phenomenology and schizoanalysis is often stark, scholars have underlined this in a number of ways, citing the "radical distinction" between the account given of subjectivity and that of the noesis-noema poles, and the "inertial" shut-in transcendental subject, and the like.²³ Yet Guattari returns to concepts such as intentionality, only to outflank the subject–object relation, in favor of the analysis of animism, psychosis, and infantile transitivism. It is fair to say that Guattari does not expel phenomenology from his theoretical edifice, but uses it as a foil, distancing himself from "Being with a capital B," and recognizing the fragility of all existensifying functions.²⁴ The *Parmenides* may serve, then, as a loop line around the tradition of fecund exchanges between the Germans and the ancient Greeks.

The Foreword provides a detailed contextualization of Guattari's scholarly source materials that grounded his interest in Parmenides and early philosophy, and how the ontological problem of the one and the many may be situated in the context of his collaborations with Gilles Deleuze. The source text and translations present in succession the French original handwritten pages, the French transcription by Stéphane Nadaud, followed by the English, Spanish, Japanese, German, Polish, and Russian translations. We included Guattari's original handwriting in order to provide visible evidence of the existensifying dimension of analogue production in the form of small notebooks. Guattari wrote about his struggles with writing in his journals, "keeping up my penmanship, my style," among similar remarks in *The Anti-Oedipus Papers* about the task of writing alone, and the pressure of writing for Deleuze, which have been widely quoted[25]; here, however, the pressures of collaboration have receded. The traces on the pages themselves, like the metallic residue of a paper clip, the crossed-through words and phrases, the loops that indicate scene breaks and provide a graphical refrain throughout the text, right down to a misnumbered page, display Guattari's playful affinity with dialog, until the final section fragments and it is sometimes not clear who is speaking. The final sentence indicating a voice-over "Do not reply to … [?]" sends us into a hors-champ, perhaps Guattari's own voice, which, we hope in a completion fantasy, might provide some context for the appearance and behavior of the goddess. There are gradations of raunchiness that the translators probe, and the desiring-assemblage is well served by Slavic variations on this theme.

The final part of this volume contains reference texts. The first, by Flore Garcin-Marrou, on Guattari's playwriting explains the breadth of his activity in this domain, and brings into focus the archival record of documents. We include an updated existing English translation of Guattari's play *Socrates* as a key text for understanding the humor of his approach to ancient philosophy. Guattari's plays have not been discussed as widely as his screenplay, *A Love of UIQ*,[26] which is one among other works for film and television that he wrote, pursuing his love of science fiction, and his molecular version of Kafka that would be a made-for television film, perhaps, he hoped, and result in a "series" for a prestige television platform.[27] While *UIQ* remains unrealized, *Kafka's Dreams* (based on Guattari's collection of sixty-five dreams of Kafka)[28] was directed by Philippe Adrien in 1984 (at Ivry) and then revived in 1985 (at Vincennes); and *Socrates*, that "pataphysical parable,"[29] was staged by Enzo Cormann in 1988 (in Paris), and featured a schizophrenic named Georges who believes he is the great ancient Greek dialectician. Cormann repeatedly emphasized the "schoolboy" element of Guattari's theatrical vision, and cultivated some of Guattari's fascination with portable cassette tape recorders, which he used in his analytic sessions, utilizing one on stage as a source of sound effects. The cosmic and the comic meet in the figure of the chaosmic artisan, the one who plunges into chaos only to resurface bearing enriched complex components for subjectivation.

Notes

1. In particular, of course, the *Parmenides*. Overall, Guattari's unpublished preparatory manuscript notes for *Qu'est-ce que la philosophie ?* (IMEC GRT 41.21–37), as well as some of his texts from 1990 to 1992, witness, though, to his growing interest in early Greek philosophy, more broadly.

2. Jean Voilquin (ed. and trans.), *Les Penseurs grecs avant Socrate. De Thalès de Milet à Prodicos*, Paris: Garnier/Flammarion, 1964.

3. Félix Guattari, *Schizoanalytic Cartographies*, trans. Andrew Goffey, London: Bloomsbury, 2013, 275 n. 2.

4. Ibid., 173.

5. Ibid., 178.

6. Ibid., 173.

7. In a 1992 interview, titled "Chaosmose, vers une nouvelle sensibilité," with Kuniichi Uno, Guattari praises the pre-Socratic philosophers: "*Ils ne tendent pas vers cette espèce de pôle d'abolition chaosmique qu'est l'Être. Ils vont vers la qualité, ils vont vers la multiplicité. Ils vont vers le récit* "[They don't tend towards that sort of pole of chaosmic abolition that is Being. They move towards quality, towards multiplicity—towards narrative] (*Qu'est-ce que l'écosophie ?*, ed. Stéphane Nadaud, Paris: Lignes/IMEC, 2018, 87). Compare this with his advocacy elsewhere (ibid., 103, 291, 300) of a "cartographic" ontology sensible to "heterogeneity," and thus non-univocal—*contra* Heidegger, one may safely infer, regardless of his otherwise positive appraisal of Heidegger's willingness to think Being beyond its "actuality" (in *Schizoanalytic Cartographies*, 91) and of Heidegger's Fourfold (in his unpublished notes for *Qu'est-ce que la philosophie ?*, in particular IMEC GTR 41.21 and 41.31); but perhaps too, despite his acknowledgment of Deleuze's intensive ontology, *pace* Deleuze (see in this respect Guattari's Leibnizian reservations, in *The Anti-Oedipus Papers*, ed. Stéphane Nadaud, trans. Kélina Gotman, Los Angeles, CA: Semiotext(e), 2006, 254–79, toward

Deleuze's exclusively Spinozist ontology)? Assuredly, Deleuze's ontology asserts the positiveness of the singular, but it simultaneously sacrifices it on the altar of Being's oneness, thereby echoing Heidegger's "ontological difference," which Deleuze makes his, together with Heidegger's "univocist" ontology, in *Difference and Repetition*, trans. Paul Patton, New York: Columbia University Press, 1994, ix, 64–6—in addition to positing Parmenides as the latter's ultimate source (ibid., 35).

8   Voilquin, *Les Penseurs*, 91.

9   Ibid., 95.

10 See, e.g., as regards his interpretation of Parmenides thereof, Heidegger, *Early Greek Thinking*, trans. David Farrel Krell and Frank A. Capuzzi, San Francisco, CA: Harper & Row, 1984, 79–101.

11 Hanjo Berressem, *Félix Guattari's Schizoanalytic Ecology*, Edinburgh: Edinburgh University Press, 2021, 150.

12 Guattari, *Schizoanalytic Cartographies*, 178.

13 Cf. *The Anti-Oedipus Papers*, 391: 'Being as such [*l'être en soi*], the being unit [*l'être unité*], being as the essence of the same, are the contingencies of disempowered enunciation. So we have to reverse the alternative: connection of existing flows and disjunction of representative [or enunciative] chains, to end up seizing the conjunction of processes as a [...] synthesis which [...] opens up onto the opposition between being and representation' (i.e., between being and enunciation). Arguably, Guattari's use of Parmenides in *Schizoanalytic Cartographies* fulfills such project from a standpoint that proves at once ontological and temporal (unary time, time as the essence of the same ... etc.). On Guattari's concept of a "plane of consistency," see n. 22 below.

14 Aristotle, *Physics* 184aff and *Metaphysics* 986bff. In *The Basic Works*, ed. Richard McKeon, New York: Random House, 1941. Notice, however, that in Plato's *Sophist* 254b–259d, "Being" already becomes a dimension permanently crossed by four other dimensions (to wit, "sameness," "otherness," "stillness," and "becoming"), which makes of it a constantly interfered thing or issue, among others.

15 Gilles Deleuze and Félix Guattari, *A Thousand Plateaus*, trans. Brian Massumi, Minneapolis, MN: University of Minnesota Press, 1987, 43.

16 Gilles Deleuze and Félix Guattari, *Kafka: Toward a Minor Literature*, trans. Dana Polan, Minneapolis, MN: University of Minnesota Press, 1985, 5.

17 Jacques Lacan, *Encore 1972–73 Book XX: The Seminar of Jacques Lacan*, trans. Bruce Fink, New York: W.W. Norton, 1998, 118.

18 Ibid., 114.

19 Ibid., 22.

20 Alain Badiou, "Lacan and the Presocratics," in *Lacan: The Silent Partners*, ed. Slavoj Zizek, London: Verso, 2006, 9.

21 Indeed, Guattari's earliest approach to the problem of the One and the Many is found in a 1961–6 letter to Lacan ("From One Sign to the Other") partly included in *Psychanalysis and Transversality*, trans. A. Hodges, Los Angeles, CA: Semiotext(e), 2015, 179–205. Guattari employs there a binary code (+, −) and its possible combinations to illustrate how three phonemes (i.e., several heterogeneous elements thus formally unified, for they can be similarly transcribed and thus become one) can be variously connected to produce different enunciation effects (ibid., 189–90), and hence how "One and Multiple" (201), how a unifying code and its diverging dynamic effects, can be said to interact to thereby clarify the status of what he calls desire's (many) "point-signs" (ibid., 181). In *Cartographies Schizoanalytiques*, p. 120–1, figs. 2, 4, and 5, Guattari uses a similar code (o, −) to depict how any non-yet-vectorized elements disseminated through reality's primordial (and unary) chaotic milieu or Brownian dispersion, achieve subsequent degrees of "determinability" and "consistency" (ibid., 119–27; cf. his definition of being as "modulation of consistency" in ibid., 107). Like in 1961–6, therefore, the question at stake for Guattari in the late 1980s is the relation between the One and the Many, two terms whose respective sign-avatars Guattari had described in 1971 as a "disjoint couple"—French: "*couple disjoint*" (*Écrits pour L'Anti-Œdipe*, ed. Stéphane Nadaud, Paris: Lignes/Manifeste, 2004, 394), an expression which the English translation of Guattari's preparatory notes for *Anti-Oedipus* oversimplifies by rendering it as "pair" (*The Anti-Oedipus Papers*, 278).

22 Guattari's 1971 qualification of the One and the Many as a "disjoint couple" (on which, see the previous note) is a crucial one indeed for understanding what, regardless of their shared concerns and fruitful collaboration, separates Guattari from Deleuze in philosophical terms. For it shows that, originally, Guattari thought of the One and the Many in chiastic or inverted-proportional terms—more, then, like Heraclitus, for whom (in frags. DK B8, B32, B41, B50, B51, B53, B54, B60, B62, B65, B72, B88, B91b, B108, B123, etc.) the unity of opposites (their being brought together) amounts to their disjunctive synthesis or Difference *qua* thinkable event (on which, see Clémence Ramnoux, *Œuvres*, vol. 1, 195–617, esp.

195, 198–205, 414, 441, 447, and Maurice Blanchot's Preface therein, 183–93), than Parmenides, for whom being's Unity underlies the Many in essentialist terms (cf. Parmenides, frag. DK B4; Aristotle, *Metaphysics* 983b 6-18; Emanuele Severino, *The Essence of Nihilism*, ed. Ines Testoni and Alessandro Carrera, trans. Giacomo Donis, London: Verso, 2016, 45–135). And unlike Deleuze who, *more Spinoziano*, tends to think the One as an underlying substance, as well—in somewhat conventional terms from the viewpoint of the history of philosophy. Thus, for example, when, in his seminar on Spinoza of March 24, 1981, Deleuze realizes that interpreting the One as the Many's substance or being could lead back to pantheism, he limits himself to rework as a possible escape route from the medieval distinction between (one) existence and (many) essences by superimposing onto it his own distinction (which he had advanced in 1968 in *Difference and Repetition*, 36: "differences do not have the same essence," yet "do not change being's [single] essence") between (one) "Being" and (many) "essences": there is "equality of Being for unequal essences," he affirms ("Spinoza: The Velocities of Thought," Part 3, l. 6 from the bottom, in response to a question formulated by Anne Querrien). Conversely, in Guattari the One is at once topological ("*plane* of consistency") and ideal: "The plane of consistency is an *Idea*," writes Guattari in 1972, "that integrates the set of all powers of the disjoined" (*The Anti-Oedipus Papers*, 395, emphasis added, but the capitalization of the word "idea" is Guattari's own). For Deleuze, however, Being is not just idea, even if it is "said" of what differs (*Difference and Repetition*, 36): it is, following Spinoza, one and a single substance (absolute for that matter, as he writes in *Expressionism in Philosophy*, trans. Martin Joughin, New York: Zone Books, 1992, 197) with different modes. "[S]ubstance pluralism (*le pluralisme des substances*)," Guattari claims instead in 1971, "is our business" (ibid., 260). In rigor, Deleuze only comes close to Guattari's topological understanding of the One with his notion of a "nomadic space" (*Difference and Repetition*, 36–7), but ends up transforming it (if one leaves aside the plateau on the "smooth" and the "striated" in *A Thousand Plateaus*) into the notion of a desert-like abyss where differences are ultimately erased on behalf of a sacrificial ethics (*Essays Critical and Clinical*, 1, 115–16; cf. the theme of the abyss in *Difference and Repetition*, 28–9, 112, 258, 276). And just like one can find, in Deleuze and Guattari's joint writings, passages that bespeak Deleuze's influence in matters of ontology and henology (e.g., the statement that there is a "single divine substance" for all differences in *Anti-Oedipus*, 309), so one can find other passages that betray Guattari's influence (e.g., the view that "the elements or parts of the desiring-machines […] must not be [viewed as] […] the differentiations of a single being, but [as] different or really-distinct things, [i.e., as] distinct 'beings' […] [like] the clover and the bee," which is paradoxically put forward too in vol. 1 of *Capitalism and Schizophrenia*, 323).

23   Paul Bains, "Subjectless Subjectivities," in *A Shock to Thought*, ed. Brian Massumi, London and New York: Routledge, 2002, 105.

24   Examples are distributed throughout his final book, *Chaosmosis*, trans. Paul Bains and Julian Pefanis, Bloomington, IN: Indiana University Press, 1995. See Genosko, "The Quandaries of Machinic Subjectivity in Félix Guattari's *Chaosmosis*," in *Technology, Urban Space and the Networked Community*, eds. Saswat Das and Ananya Roy Pratihar, Delhi: Palgrave Macmillan, 2022, 71–103; and Segovia, "Guattari \Heidegger: On Quaternities, Deterritorialisation, and Worlding," *Delezue and Guattari Studies* 16/4 (2022): 508–22.

25   Félix Guattari, *The Anti-Oedipus Papers*, trans. Kélina Gotman, New York and Los Angeles, CA: Semiotexte, 2002, 404.

26   Félix Guattari, *A Love of UIQ*, trans. Silvia Maglioni and Graeme Thomson, Minneapolis, MN: Univocal, 2012.

27   Félix Guattari, "Project for a Film by Kafka, trans Jakub Zdebik," *Deleuze Studies* 3/2 (2009): 150–61.

28   Félix Guattari, *Soixante-cinq Rêves de Franz Kafka*, ed. Stéphane Nadaud, Fécamp: Lignes, 2007.

29   Flore Garcin-Marrou and Enzo Cormann, "Félix Guattari, Chaosmic Playwright," *Chimères* 77/2 (2012): 158–72.

References

Aristotle, *The Basic Works*, ed. Richard McKeon, New York: Random House, 1941.
Badiou, Alain, "Lacan and the Pre-Socratics," in *Lacan: The Silent Partners*, ed. Slavoj Zizek, London: Verso, 2006, 7–16.
Bains, Paul, "Subjectless Subjectivities," in *A Shock to Thought*, ed. Brian Massumi, London and New York: Routledge, 2002, 101–16.
Blanchot, Maurice, "Préface" to Clémence Ramnoux, *Héraclite, l'homme entre les choses et les mots*, in Clémence Ramnoux, *Œuvres*, eds. Rossella Saetta Cottone and Alexandre Marcinkowski, 2 vols., Paris: Les Belles Letres, 2020, vol. 1, 183–93.

Berressem, Hanjo, *Félix Guattari's Schizoanalytic Ecology*, Edinburgh: Edinburgh University Press, 2021.
Deleuze, Gilles, *Expressionism in Philosophy: Spinoza*, trans. Martin Joughin, New York: Zone Books, 1992.
Deleuze, Gilles, *Difference and Repetition*, trans. Paul Patton, New York: Columbia University Press, 1994.
Deleuze, Gilles, *Essays Critical and Clinical*, trans. Daniel W. Smith and Michael A. Greco, London: Verso, 1998.
Deleuze, Gilles, "Spinoza: The Velocities of Thought," March 24, 1981, trans. Timothy S. Murphy and Charles J. Stivale (2020), *The Deleuze Seminars*, available at: https://deleuze.cla.purdue.edu/lecture/lecture-14-0/
Deleuze, Gilles, and Félix Guattari, *Anti-Oedipus: Capitalism and Schizophrenia*, trans. Robert Hurley, Mark Seem, and Helen R. Lane, Foreword by Michel Foucault, London: Continuum, 1983.
Deleuze, Gilles, and Félix Guattari, *Kafka: Toward a Minor Literature*, trans. Dana Polan, Minneapolis, MN: University of Minnesota Press, 1985.
Deleuze, Gilles, and Félix Guattari, *A Thousand Plateaus*, trans. Brian Massumi, Minneapolis, MN: University of Minnesota Press, 1987.
Garcin-Marrou, Flore, and Enzo Cormann, "Félix Guattari, Chaosmic Playwright," *Chimères* 77/2 (2012): 158–72.
Genosko, Gary, "The Quandaries of Machinic Subjectivity in Félix Guattari's *Chaosmosis*," in *Technology, Urban Space and the Networked Community*, eds. Saswat Das and Ananya Roy Pratihar, Delhi: Palgrave Macmillan, 2022, 71–103.
Guattari, Félix, *Chaosmosis*, trans. Paul Bains and Julian Pefanis, Bloomington, IN: Indiana University Press, 1995.
Guattari, Félix, *Écrits pour L'Anti-Œdipe*, ed. Stéphane Nadaud, Paris: Lignes/Manifest, 2004.
Guattari, Félix. *The Anti-Oedipus Papers*, ed. Stéphane Nadaud, trans. Kélina Gotman, Los Angeles, CA: Semiotext(e), 2006.
Guattari, Félix, *Soixante-cinq Rêves de Franz Kafka*, ed. Stéphane Nadaud, Fécamp: Lignes, 2007.
Guattari, Félix, "Project for a Film by Kafka, trans Jakub Zdebik," *Deleuze Studies* 3/2 (2009): 150–61.
Guattari, Félix, *A Love of UIQ*, trans. Silvia Maglioni and Graeme Thomson, Minneapolis, MN: Univocal, 2012.
Guattari, Félix, *Schizoanalytic Cartographies*, trans. Andrew Goffey, London: Bloomsbury, 2013.
Guattari, Félix, *Psychoanalysis and Transversality*, trans. Ames Hodges, Introduction by G. Deleuze, Los Angeles, CA: Semiotex(e), 2015.
Guattari, Félix. *Qu'est-ce que l'écosophie ?* ed. Stéphane Nadaud, Paris: Lignes/IMEC, 2018.

Guattari, Félix. IMEC GTR 41.21–37. Unpublished manuscript notes for *Qu'est-ce que la philosophie ?* Caen. IMEC, Fonds Guattari.

Heidegger, Martin, *Early Greek Thinking*, trans. David Farrell Krell and Frank A. Capuzzi, San Francisco, CA: Harper, 1984.

Kirk G. S., J. E. Raven and M. Schofield. *The Pre-Socratic Philosophers: A Critical History with a Selection of Texts*, second edition, Cambridge: Cambridge University Press, 1983.

Lacan, Jacques, *Encore 1972–3 Book XX: The Seminar of Jacques Lacan*, trans. B. Fink, New York: W.W. Norton, 1998.

Plato, *Complete Works*, ed. John M. Cooper, Indianapolis, IN: Hackett, 1997.

Ramnoux, Clémence, *Œuvres*, ed. Rossella Saetta Cottone and Alexandre Marcinkowski, 2 vols., Paris: Les Belles Letres, 2020.

Segovia, Carlos A., "Guattari \Heidegger: On Quaternities, Deterritorialisation, and Worlding," *Deleuze and Guattari Studies* 16/4 (2022): 508–22.

Severino, Emanuele, *The Essence of Nihilism*, ed. Ines Testoni and Alessandro Carrera, trans. Giacomo Donis, London: Verso, 2016.

Voilquin, Jean (ed. and trans.), *Les Penseurs Grec Avant Socrate: De Thalès de Milet à Prodicos*, Paris: Garnier/Flammarion, 1964.

ACKNOWLEDGMENTS

We are grateful to Emmanuelle, Bruno, and Stephen Guattari for authorizing us to reproduce in facsimile Guattari's *Parménide*, and to the Institut Mémoires de l'édition contemporaine (IMEC) in Caen for providing us hi-res photographs of the manuscript pages. We are also thankful to Guattari's heirs, and to Solène Nicolas, for letting us reuse here, if slightly modified, the latter's English translation of Guattari's *Socrate*, which was originally published in 2012 in *Deleuze Studies*, vol. 6, no. 2, pp. 25–38.

This project was originally initiated by Stéphane Nadaud and we are delighted to bring it to completion, but in a different way than he envisaged, no doubt.

We are grateful for the thoughtful comments made by the reviewers of this project.

Lastly, we should like to thank all of the members of our translation team for their sterling efforts to bring to completion this multilingual edition. The team includes Carlos A. Segovia, Gary Genosko, Iloe Ariss, Mahoro Murasawa, Ben Bandosz, and Mikhail Fedorchenko, all of whom worked on *Parménide*; Jay Hetrick translated Flore Garcin-Marrou's essay, originally published in *Chimères*—we are delighted to have her permission to include it, and in addition note the assistance of Anne Querrien in securing the journal's permission. Last but not least, we acknowledge the contributions of Veniamin Gushchin and Charles Stivale, both of whom offered sage translation advice.

PART ONE

SOURCE MATERIALS AND TRANSLATIONS OF *PARMENIDES*

0
Félix Guattari, *Parménide*, Facsimile Edition

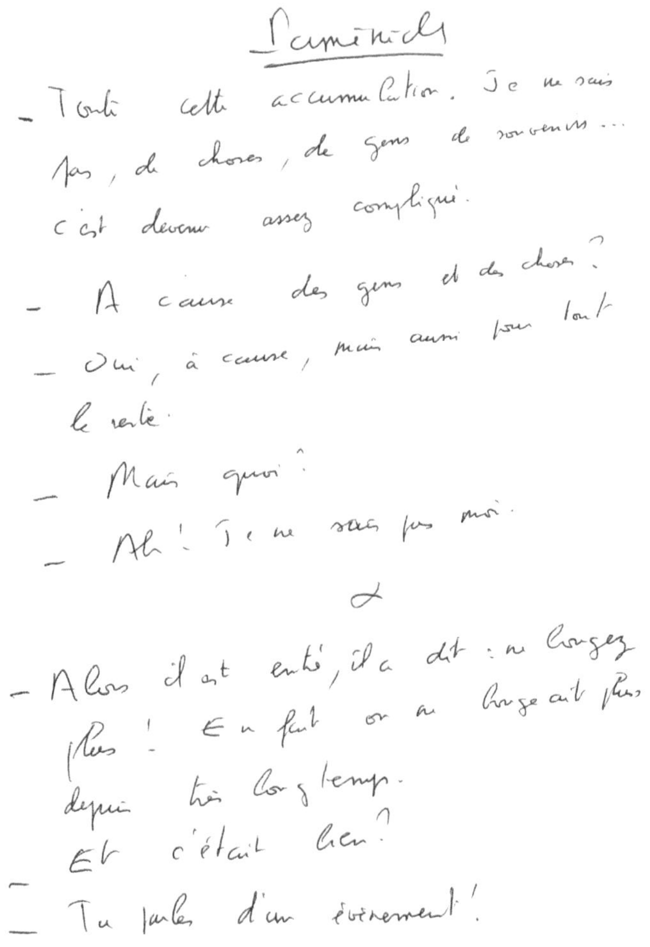

Parménide

— Toute cette accumulation. Je ne sais pas, de choses, de gens, de souvenirs... C'est devenu assez compliqué.
— À cause des gens et des choses ?
— Oui, à cause, mais aussi pour tout le reste.
— Mais quoi ?
— Ah ! Je ne sais pas moi.

∝

— Alors il est entré, il a dit : « ne bougez plus ! » En fait on ne bougeait plus depuis très longtemps.
— Et c'était bien ?
—
— Tu parles d'un événement !

FIGURE 1 *Guattari*, **Parménide** *(n.d.), IMEC, dossier GTR 22.11, p. 1.*

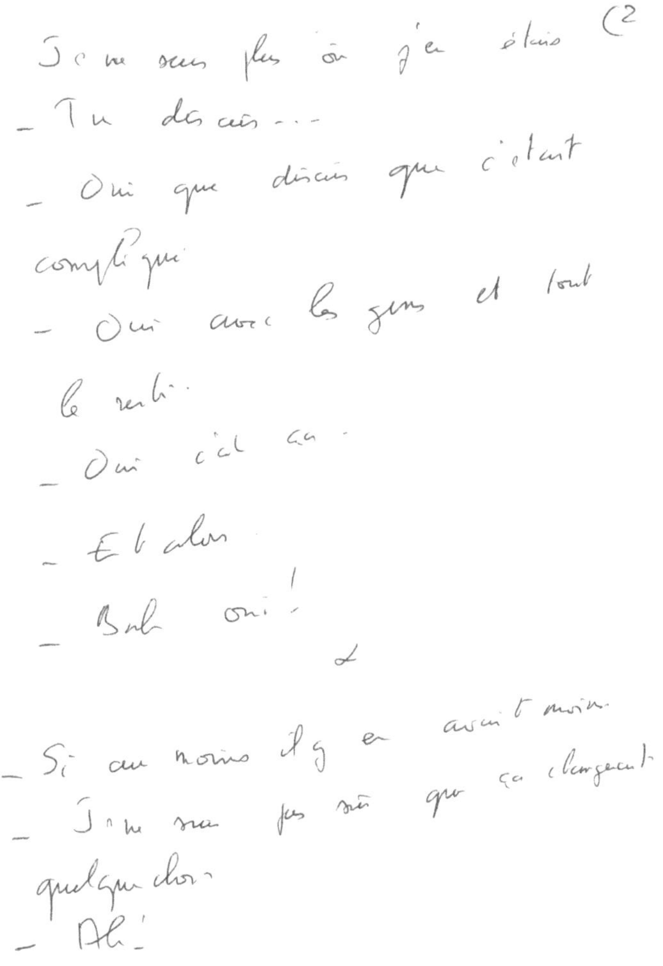

> Je ne sais plus où j'en étais (2
> — Tu disais...
> — Oui que disais que c'était compliqué
> — Oui avec les gens et tout le reste.
> — Oui c'est ça
> — Et alors
> — Bah oui !
>
> — Si au moins il y en avait moins.
> — Je ne sais pas sûr que ça changerait quelque chose
> — Ah !

FIGURE 2 Guattari, Parménide *(n.d.)*, IMEC, dossier GTR 22.11, *p. 2*.

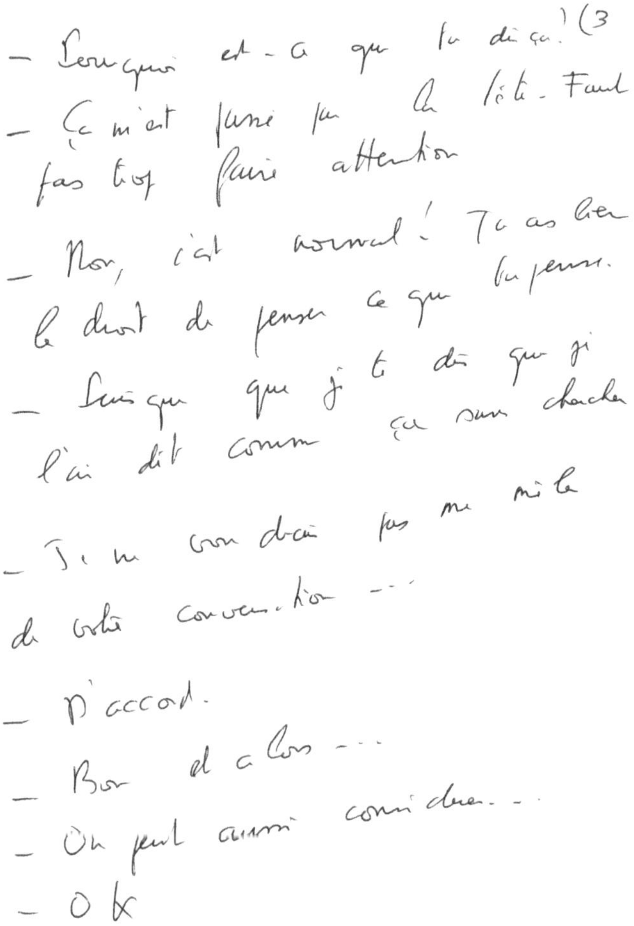

— Pourquoi est-ce que tu dis ça ? (3
— Ça m'est passé par la tête. Faut pas trop faire attention
— Non, c'est normal ! Tu as bien le droit de penser ce que tu penses.
— Puisque que je te dis que je l'ai dit comme ça sans chercher
— Je ne vous dois pas me mêle de cette conversation ...
— D'accord.
— Bon et alors ...
— On peut aussi considérer ...
— Ok

FIGURE 3 *Guattari,* Parménide *(n.d.), IMEC, dossier GTR 22.11, p. 3.*

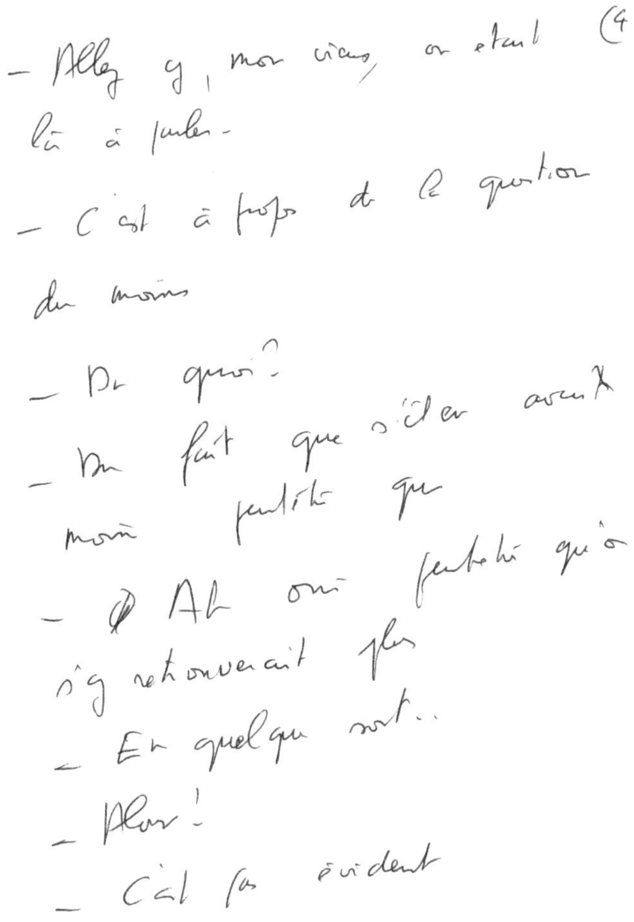

— Allez y, mon vieux, on était (4
là à parler.
— C'est à propos de la question
du moins
— De quoi?
— Du fait que s'il en avait
moins peut-être que
— Ah oui peut-être qu'on
s'y retrouverait plus
— En quelque sort...
— Plus!
— C'est pas évident

FIGURE 4 *Guattari*, Parménide *(n.d.), IMEC, dossier GTR 22.11, p. 4.*

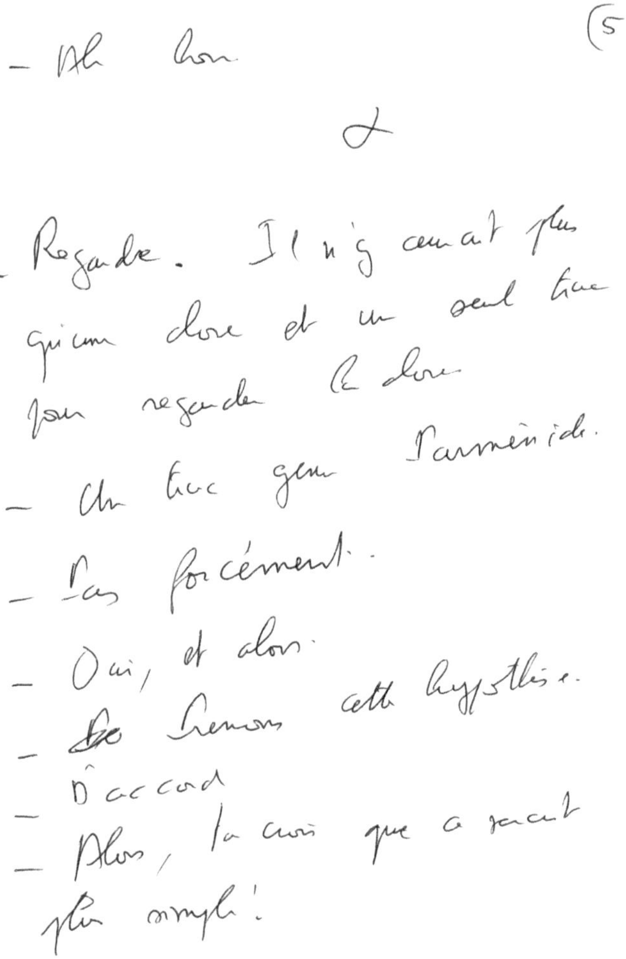

5

– Ah bon.

&

– Regarde. Il n'y aurait plus
qu'une chose et un seul être
pour regarder la chose
– Un être genre Parménide.
– Pas forcément.
– Oui, et alors.
– Prenons cette hypothèse.
– D'accord
– Alors, tu crois que ça serait
plus simple!

FIGURE 5 *Guattari,* Parménide *(n.d.), IMEC, dossier GTR 22.11, p. 5.*

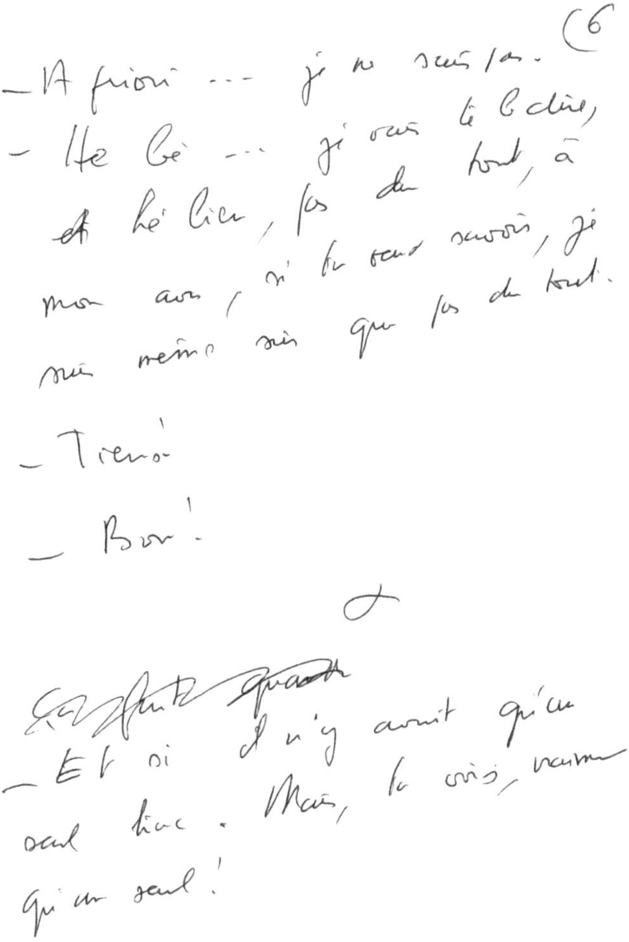

FIGURE 6 Guattari, **Parménide** (*n.d.*), *IMEC, dossier GTR*
22.11, p. 6.

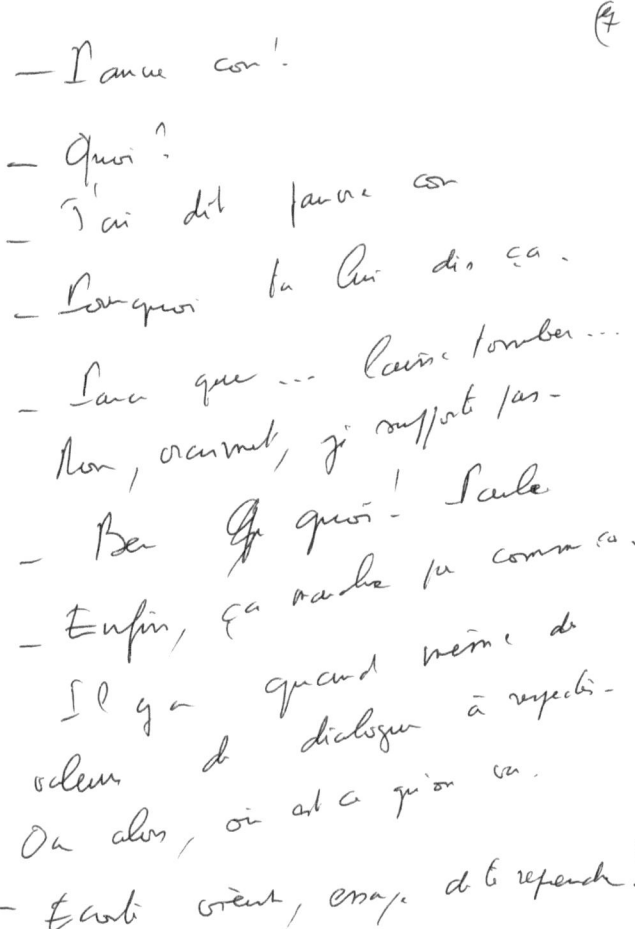

FIGURE 7 Guattari, Parménide (n.d.), IMEC, dossier GTR 22.11, p. 7.

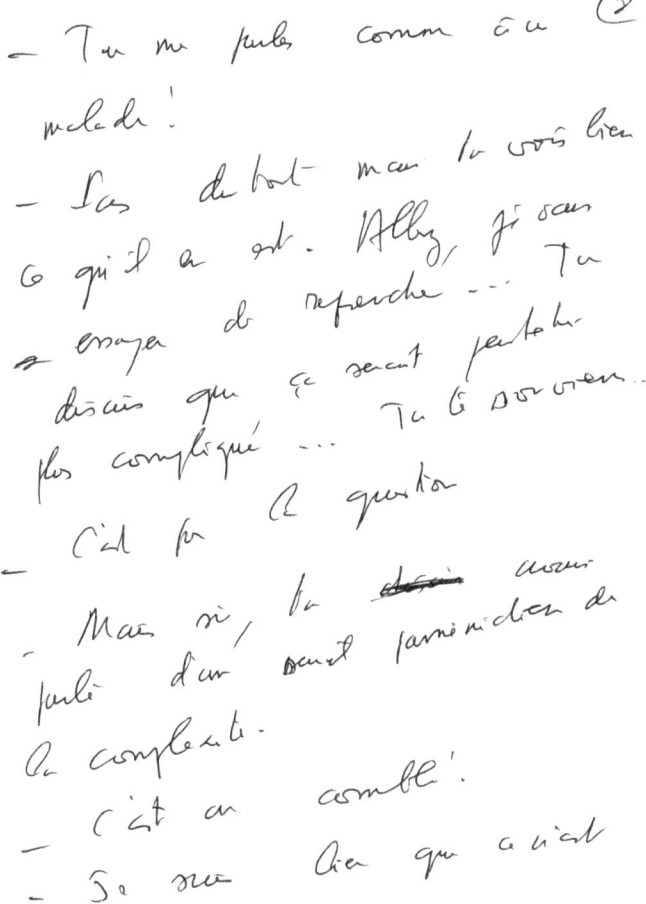

FIGURE 8 *Guattari*, **Parménide** *(n.d.)*, *IMEC, dossier GTR 22.11, p. 8.*

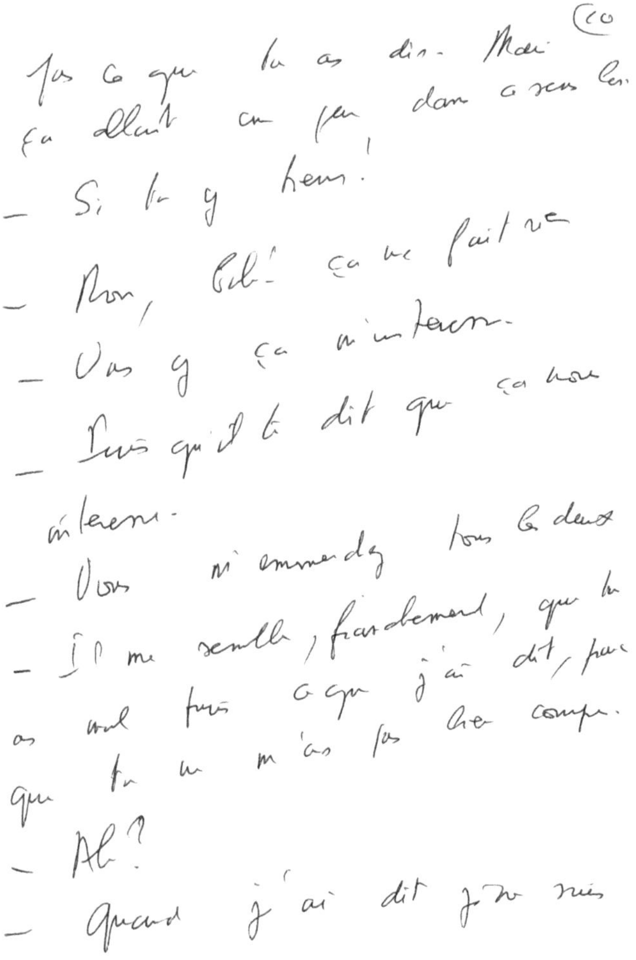

FIGURE 9 *Guattari*, Parménide *(n.d.), IMEC, dossier GTR 22.11, p. 9.*

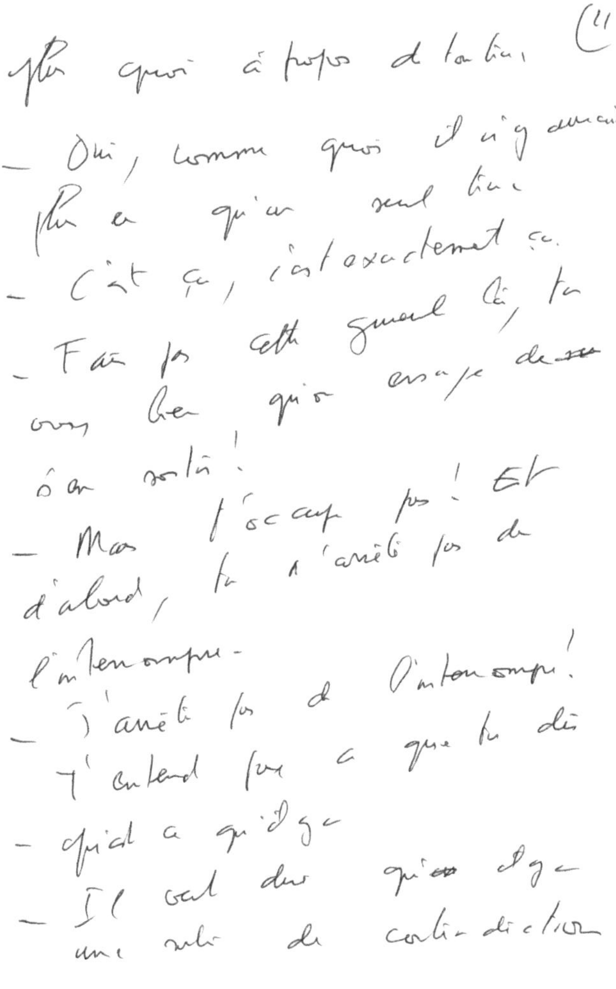

FIGURE 10 *Guattari*, **Parménide** *(n.d.), IMEC, dossier GTR 22.11, p. 10.*

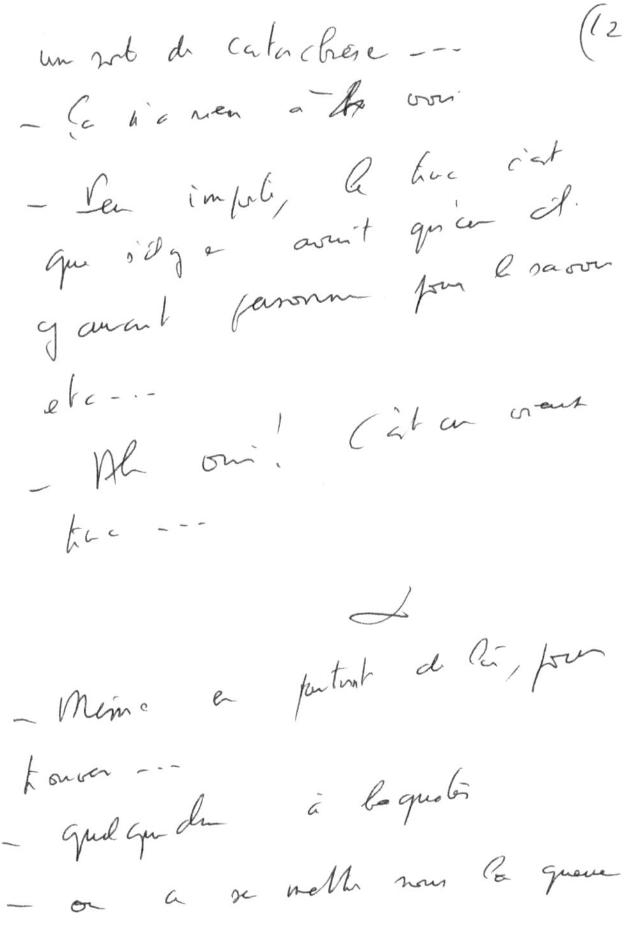

FIGURE 11 *Guattari,* Parménide *(n.d.), IMEC, dossier GTR 22.11, p. 11.*

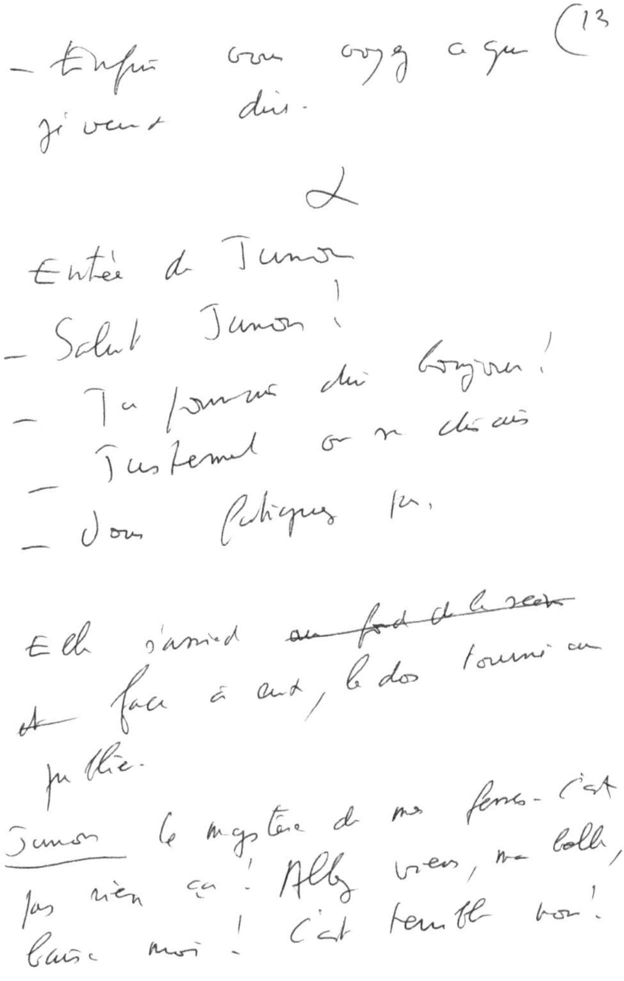

FIGURE 12 Guattari, Parménide *(n.d.)*, IMEC, dossier GTR 22.11, p. 12.

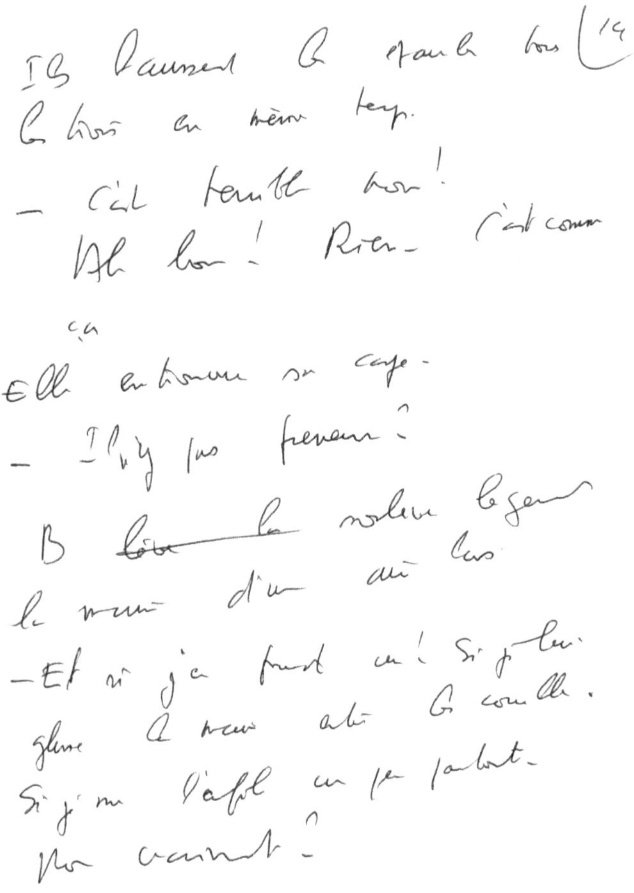

FIGURE 13 *Guattari,* Parménide *(n.d.), IMEC, dossier GTR 22.11, p. 13.*

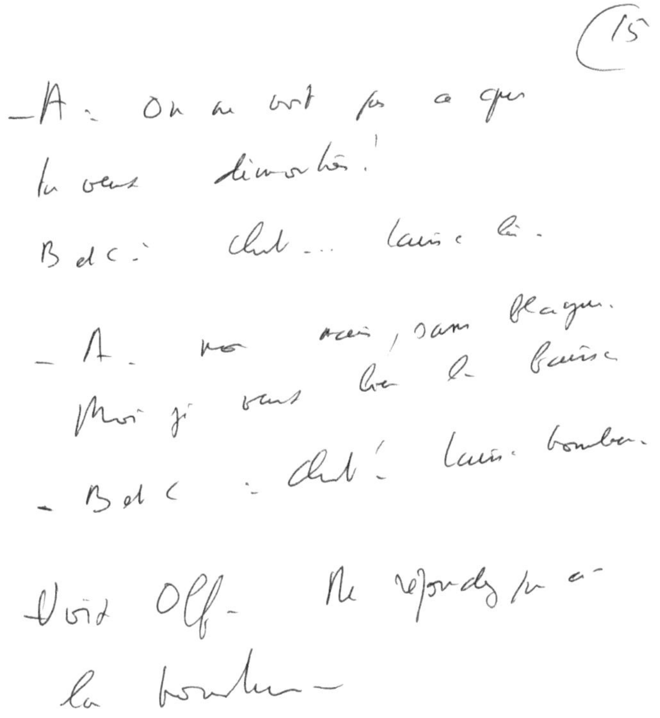

FIGURE 14 *Guattari,* **Parménide** *(n.d.), IMEC, dossier GTR 22.11, p. 14.*

1

French

Transcribed by Stéphane Nadaud

(1) Parménide

— Toute cette accumulation. Je me [ne] sais pas, de choses, de gens de souvenirs … c'est devenu assez compliqué.
— A cause des gens et des choses ?
— Oui, à cause, mais aussi pour tout le reste.
— Mais quoi ?
— Ah ! Je ne sais pas moi.

* * *

— Alors il est entré, il a dit : ne bougez plus ! En fait on ne bougeait plus depuis très longtemps.
— Et c'était bien ?
— Tu parles d'un événement ! (2) Je ne sais plus où j'en étais
— Tu disais …
— Oui que [je] disais que c'était compliqué.
— Oui avec les gens et tout le reste.

— Oui c'est ça.

— Et alors

— Bah oui !

✶ ✶ ✶

— Si au moins il y en avait moins.

— Je ne suis pas sûr que ça changerait quelque chose

— Ah!

(3)— Pourquoi est-ce que tu dis ça ?

— Ça m'est passé par la tête. Faut pas faire attention

— Non, c'est normal ! Tu as bien le droit de penser ce que tu penses.

— Puisque que je te dis que je l'ai dit comme ça sans chercher

— Je ne voudrais pas me mêler de votre conversation …

— D'accord.

— Bon et alors …

— On peut aussi considérer …

— Ok

(4)— Allez y, mon vieux, on était là à parler.

— C'est à propos de la question du moins.

— Du quoi ?

— Du fait que s'il en avait moins peut-être que

— ◻ Ah oui peut-être qu'on n'y retrouverait plus

— En quelque sorte …

— Alors !

— C'est pas evident

(5)— Ah bon.

* * *

— Regarde. Il n'y aurait plus qu'une chose et un seul truc pour regarder la chose

— Un truc genre Parmènide

— Pas forcément.

— Oui, et alors.

— P̶ Prenons cette hypothèse.

— D'accord

— Alors, tu crois que ce serait plus simple !

(6)— A priori … je ne sais pas.

— Hé bé … je vais te le dire. Hé bien, pas de tout, à mon avis, si tu veux savoir, je suis même sûr que pas de tout

— Tiens !

— Bon !

* * *

~~Ça fut qua~~

— Et si il n'y avait qu'un seul truc. Mais, tu vois, vraiment qu'un seul !

(7)— Pauvre con !

— Quoi ?

— J'ai dit pauvre con

— Pourquoi tu le dis ça ?

— Parce que … laisse tomber … Non, vraiment, je supporte pas—

— Bien ▯ quoi ! Parle

— Enfin, ça marche pas comme ça. Il y a quand même des valeurs de dialogue à respecter— Ou alors, où est ce qu'on va (?)

— Ecoute vieux, essaye de te reprendre !

(8)— Tu me parles comme à un malade.

— Pas du tout mais tu vois bien ce qu'il en est. Allez je vais essayer de reprendre … Tu disais que ça serait peut être plus compliqué. Tu te souviens …
— C'est pas la question
— Mais si, tu ~~disais~~ avais parlé d'un seuil parménidien de la complexité.
— C'est un comble !
— Je sais bien que ce n'est (10) pas ce que tu as dit. Mais ça allait un peu dans ce sens là.
— Si tu y tiens !
— Non, bah ça ne fait rien
— Vas-y ça m'intéresse
— Puis qu'il te dit que ça nous intéresse.
— Vous m'emmerdez tous les deux
— Il me semble, franchement, que tu as mal pris ce que j'ai dit, parce que tu ne m'as pas bien compris.
— Ah ?
— Quand j'ai dit je ne sais (11) plus quoi à propos de ton truc.
— Oui, comme quoi il n'y avait plus ◻ qu'un seul truc.
— C'est ça, c'est exactement ça.
— Fait pas cette gueule là, tu vois bien qu'on essaye de bien sortir !
— Mais t'occupe pas ! Et d'abord tu n'arrêtes pas de l'interrompre.
— J'arrête pas de l'interrompre ! Tu entends pas ce que tu dis
— Qu'est-ce qu'il y a (?)
— Il veut dire qu'il y a une sorte de contradiction (12) une sorte de catachrèse …
— Ça n'a rien à ◻ voir
— Peu importe, le truc c'est que s'il y avait qu'un il y aurait personne pour le savoir etc …

— Ah oui ! C'est un vieux truc ...

* * *

— Même en partant de là, pour trouver ...
— Quelque chose à béqueter
— On a se mettre sous la queue
(13)— Enfin vous voyez ce que je veux dire ?

* * *

Entré de Junon.
— Salut Junon !
— Tu pourrais dire bonjour !
— Justement on se disais [sic]
— Vous fatiguez pas.
Elle s'assied ~~au fond de la scène et~~ face à eux, le dos tourné au public
— (Junon) Le mystère de mes fesses. C'est pas rien ça ! Allez viens, ma belle, baise moi ! C'est terrible non !
(14) Ils haussent les épaules tous les trois en même temps.
— C'est terrible non !
Ah bon ! Rien. C'est comme ça
Elle entrouvre sa cage.
— Il n'y a pas preneur ?
B ~~lève le~~ soulève légèrement la main d'un air las
— Et si j'en ◻ un! Si je lui glisse la main entre les couilles. Si je me l'affole un peu partout. Non vraiment ?
(15)— A : On ne voit pas ce que tu veux démontrer !
B et C : chut ... laisse là.
— A : non mais, sans blague. Moi je veux bien la baiser

B et C : chut! laisse tomber.

VOIX OFF. Ne répondez pas à la ◻ {provocation}

NB. *Ed. note.* The absence of manuscript p. 9. does not disrupt the flow of the dialogue. The incomplete words and phrases originally crossed out by Guattari are reproduced in the transcription. ◻ stands for an undecipherable letter or set of letters, while { } stands for a conjecture.

2

English

Translated by Gary Genosko

(1) *Parmenides*[1]

— All this buildup. I don't know, of things, of memories of people … it's become rather complicated.
— Because of the people and things?
— Yes, because of them, but also for everything else as well.
— But what?
— Oh! I don't know really.

✱✱✱

— Then he came in, and said: stop moving! In actual fact, we hadn't moved for quite a while.
— And that was ok?
— You're speaking of an event! (2) I've lost where I was at.
— You were saying …
— Yes, I was saying it was complicated.
— Yes, with the people and everything else.

— That's right.

— So.

— Well, yeh!

★★★

— If at least there was less.

— I'm not sure that it would change anything.

— Ah!

— (3) Why do you say that?

— It just occurred to me. No need to pay attention.

— No, it's normal! You have the right to think what you think.

— Since I'm telling you that I said it like that without trying.

— I wouldn't want to interfere in your conversation ….

— All right.

— Well, good, so.

— One might also consider …

— Ok.

— (4) Come on pal, we're here to talk.

— It's about the question of less.

— What?

— About the fact that if perhaps there were less …

— Yes, perhaps that we wouldn't be there anymore.

— In some respect …

— In that case!

— It is not certain.

— (5) Oh, ok.

★★★

— Consider. There would only be one thing and one way only to consider the thing.

— A Parmenides-type thing (*truc*).

— Not necessarily.

— Well, and then.

— Let's consider this hypothesis.

— Fine.

— So, you think it would be simpler!

(6)— *A priori*, I don't know.

— Well … I'm going to say it to you. Well, not at all, in my view, if you want to know, I am even certain that it would not be at all.

— Really!

— Good!

***

— And if there were only one thing. But, you see, truly just one!

— (7) Poor bastard!

— What?

— I said poor bastard.

— Why do you say that?

— Because … never mind … No, truly, I can't bear …

— Well, what! Speak.

— Well, it doesn't work like that. There are still the values of dialogue to respect.—Or else, where do we go from here?

— Listen to me pal, get hold of yourself!

— (8) You talk to me like I'm ill.

— Not at all, but you can see what the point is. Let me try to start over … You said maybe it might be more complicated. You remember …

— That's not the question.
— But yes, it is, you had spoken of a parmenidean threshold of complexity.
— Give me a break!
— I'm aware that it's not (10) what you said. But it was going in that direction.
— If you say so!
— No, well, it doesn't matter.
— Go ahead, now I'm interested.
— Next he'll say it interests us.
— Both of you are pissing me off.
— It seems to me, frankly, that you have taken what I said the wrong way, because you failed to understand me.
— Oh?
— When I said I no longer (11) follow what you were saying about your thing (*truc*).
— Yes, as if there was merely a single thing.
— That's it. That is exactly it.
— Don't pout, you can see that we are trying to move forward.
— Don't you worry! And first of all, you keep interrupting.
— I can't stop interrupting. You are not listening to what you are saying.
— What's the matter?
— He means that there is a kind of contradiction (12), a catachresis of sorts …
— That has nothing to do with it.
— No matter, the thing is that if there was only one, there would not be anyone to know it, etc.
— Ah, right, it's an ancient issue (*truc*) …

***

— Even starting from there, in order to find …

— Something to nibble on.

— We have to get back in line …

(13)— Well, you see what I mean?

***

— Juno enters.

— Greetings Juno!

— You could say hello.

— We were just saying.

— Save your breath.

She sits facing them, with her back to the audience.

— (Juno) The mystery of my ass. It's not nothing! Come on, baby, fuck me. It's terrific, no!

(14) Together, all three of them shrug their shoulders.

— It's great, no?

    Oh well! Nothing. That's how it goes.

She opens her wrap (*cage*).

— Any takers?

B wearily lifts his hand

— And if I had one! If I slide my hand between the balls … if I spin my hands around … a bit allover … no really … ?

(14)— A. We cannot see what you are demonstrating … !

B and C: Wait, leave it there.

— A: no but, no joking. I want to do her ….

B and C: shh, let it rest.

Voice-over: Do not reply to …

Note

1. I am grateful for the comments of Iloe Ariss, Ben Bandosz, and Charles Stivale on my translation. All errors remain my own.

3

Spanish

Translated by Carlos A. Segovia

(1) Parménides

— Toda esta acumulación. No sé, de cosas, personas, recuerdos ... se ha vuelto muy complicada.
— ¿Por las personas y las cosas?
— Por ellas y por lo todo demás.
— ¿El qué?
— ¡Ah! No sé.[1]

***

— Entonces entró y dijo: ¡no os mováis más! De hecho, no nos movíamos desde hacía mucho.[2]
— ¿Y eso era bueno?
— ¡Hablas de un acontecimiento! (2) No recuerdo por dónde iba[3]
— Decías ...
— Sí, decía que es complicado

— Sí, por la gente y todo lo demás.

— Eso es, sí.

— ¿Y bien?

— ¡Pues eso!

★★★

— Si al menos hubiera menos …

— No estoy seguro de que eso cambiara nada

— ¡Ah!

(3)— ¿Por qué dices eso?

— Me ha venido a la cabeza. No hagas mucho caso

— ¡No, es normal! Tienes derecho a pensar lo que piensas.

— Te digo que lo he dicho así, sin buscarlo.

— No querría interferir en lo que decís[4] …

— De acuerdo.

— Bien, ¿y entonces? …

— Podríamos considerar también …

— Vale.

(4)— Venga, tío, estábamos hablando

— Es acerca de la cuestión del «menos».[5]

— ¿Cómo?

— Que si hubiera menos quizá entonces

— Ah sí, quizá ya no nos las veríamos con nada «más»[6]

— De algún modo …

— ¡Luego entonces!

— No, no es evidente

(5)— Vaya

★★★

— Mira. No habría más que una sola cosa[7] y un único truco[8] para poder verla[9]

— Un truco tipo Parménides.

— No necesariamente.

— Bueno, ¿y qué?

— Partamos de esa hipótesis.

— De acuerdo

— ¡Tú crees que todo sería más simple así!

(6)— A priori … no lo sé.

— Pues bien … voy a decírtelo, no lo sería en absoluto, no lo creo, y si quieres que te lo diga, en realidad estoy seguro de que no lo sería.

— ¡Caramba!

— ¡Así es!

★★★

— ¿Y si no hubiera más que una sola cosa[10] para todo? ¡Una solo, eh!

(7)— ¡Pobre imbécil!

— ¿Qué?

— He dicho pobre imbécil

— ¿Por qué le has dicho eso?[11]

— Porque … déjalo … Es que no, verdaderamente no lo soporto.

— ¿El qué? Habla.

— Que no puede ser así. Hay que respetar los valores del diálogo. Si no, ¿dónde vamos a ir a parar?

— ¡Escucha, tío, trata de calmarte!

(8)— Me hablas como a un loco.

— Para nada, pero date cuenta de la situación. En fin, voy intentar retomar lo que decías … Decías que sería quizá más complicado … ¿Te acuerdas?

— Esa no es la cuestión
— Sí, hablabas de un sello parmenídeo de la complejidad.
— ¡Es el colmo!
— Ya sé que no (10^{12}) lo has dicho así. Pero ese era un poco el sentido.
— ¡Si tú lo dices!
— Bah, no importa, dejémoslo.
— No, vamos, me interesa.
— Y luego te dice que eso le interesa.
— Los dos[13] me estais jodiendo.
— Francamente, me parece que te has tomado a mal lo que he dicho porque no me has comprendido bien.
— ¿Ah sí?
— Cuando he dicho no sé (11) bien qué a propósito de tu truco.
— Sí, que es como si no hubiera más que una cosa.[14]
— Eso es, exactamente.
— No pongas esa cara, ¿no ves que estamos intentando salir de esto?
— ¡Tranquilo! Es que no paras de interrumpirlo.[15]
— ¡No paro de interrumpirlo! ¿Oyes lo que dices?
— ¿Qué pasa?
— Quiere decir que hay ahí una suerte de contradicción, (12) una suerte de catacresis…
— Eso no tiene nada que ver
— No importa, la cuestión[16] es que si no hubiera más que «uno»[17] nadie podría saberlo, etc….
— ¡Ah, sí! Es un viejo truco…

✶✶✶

— Incluso partiendo de ahí para encontrar …

— algo que picotear

— o que guardarse uno en la manga

(13)— Bueno, ya sabéis qué quiero decir.

✱✱✱

Entra Juno

— ¡Hola, Juno!

— ¡Podrías saludar!

— Estábamos diciendo

— No os canseis.

Se sienta frente a ellos, de espaldas al público.

Juno [:] El misterio de mis nalgas. ¡Eso [otro] no es nada! ¡Anda, ven, preciosa, fóllame! ¡Es terrible!, ¿no?

(14) Los tres se encogen de hombros al mismo tiempo.

— ¡Es terrible!, ¿no?

   ¡Bueno! Pues nada. Es así

Entreabre su jaula.

— ¿Nadie quiere?

B levanta ligeramente la mano con aire cansado

— ¿Y si tomo una? ¿Si deslizo mi mano entre sus bolas? ¿Si me lo enfilo por aquí y por allí? No, en serio.

(15)— A: ¡No veo qué es lo que intentas demostrar!

[—] B y C: Shh … déjala en paz.

— A: No, no bromeo. Quiero follármela.

— B y C: Shh … déjalo.

Voz en off: No respondas a la [?][18]

Notes

1   El número y la identidad de los personajes no se detalla, así como tampoco el orden en el que cada uno de ellos interviene. Al final de la pieza se habla de A, B y C, pero C únicamente interviene de manera inequívoca en la p. 14, mientras que en la p. 13 hace su aparición un cuarto personaje, el único cuyo nombre se indica expresamente: Juno. Hasta la p. 11, los personajes parecen ser únicamente dos, aunque B protesta en la p. 8 acerca de A y de un tercero sobre cuya presencia no se había ofrecido antes indicio alguno.

2   El hilo de la discusión sugiere que A, es decir, el primer personaje en intervenir en la primera escena o sección del diálogo, inicia nuevamente la conversación aquí y en la siguiente sección. En cuanto a las demás secciones, las intervenciones parecen seguir en cambio el orden natural del diálogo hasta la sexta sección: B inicia la conversación en la cuarta sección, mientras que A lo hace en la quinta. En contraste, la distribución del diálogo en la sexta sección no está clara, mientras que la séptima y última sección introduce una serie de precisiones sin precedente en el resto del diálogo, pero que sólo permiten deducir parcialmente quién habla en cada caso.

3   Falta el punto final. Mantengo aquí y en lo sucesivo la puntuación final de cada línea (o su carencia, como en este caso) tal y como figura en el original; así como el uso de mayúscula o minúscula al inicio de cada línea (véase a este respecto el final de la p. 12).

4   ¿Primera intervención de C?

5   Término no entrecomillado en el original.

6   Ibid.

7   *Chose.*

8   *Truc.*

9   Repárese en que, en francés, *le truc* («el truco») puede significar también, más imprecisamente, «la cosa» o «la cuestión». El texto juega una y otra vez con dicha ambigüedad.

10 *Truc.*

11 ¿Intervención de C?

12 La numeración de las páginas salta aquí de la 8 a la 10; es decir, falta aparentemente la p. 9. No hay, sin embargo, ninguna laguna en el texto, que continúa de manera natural de una página a la otra.

13 Es decir, A y ¿C?

14 *Truc.*

15 ¿Intervención de C? A partir de aquí, el número de interlocutores no es claro, así como tampoco el orden de las intervenciones.

16 *Truc.*

17 Término no entrecomillado en el original.

18 La palabra final del diálogo es ininteligible.

4

Japanese

Translated by Mahoro Murasawa

(1) パルメニデス

— いろんなものが積み重っている。なんだろう? 物、人、記憶……かなり複雑になってきたな。
— 人々や物のせいだろうか?
— たしかにそれらのせいもあるし、それ以外のすべてのせいでもある。
— でも、それは何だい?
— ああ、僕にもわからない。

* * *

— そのとき、彼が入ってきて「動くな」と言ったんだ!実際、僕たちは長いあいだ動かなかった。
— それでうまくいったのかね?
— 君は事件について話してるのか!(2)僕は自分がどこにいたのか、もうわからないよ。
— さっきの話だけど…。

— ああ、[僕は]複雑だと言ったんだ。
— そう、人とかいろいろすべてが。
— たしかにそうだった。
— それで、どうなんだい。
— ああ、そうだ!

　　　　　　　　＊＊＊

— せめて、もっと少なかったらいいのだけれど。
— そうだったとしても、それで何が変わるのかは自信がないな。
— ああ!
(3)— なぜ君はそんなことを言うのかね?
— 頭に浮かんだんだ。あまり気にしないでくれ。
— いや、当然のことだ。君には考えることを考える権利が十分にある。
— 僕は深く考えずにそう言ったと言ったんだ。
— 君たちの会話の邪魔をしたくないのだけれど…。
— いいよ。
— よし、じゃあ…。
— こういうふうにも考えられる…。
— いいよ。
(4)— どうぞ続けてくれ、老いた友よ。僕たちは話していたところだ。
— もっと少なかったらという問いについて。
— なんだって?
— もっと少なかったらどうなんだろうってことだよ。
— ああ、そうか。そうなればもう見つからないかもしれない。

—ある意味では … 。
—おい!
—そうとも限らないよ。
(5)— まあね。

★ ★ ★

— 見てごらん。何かが見えるとしたら、もうたったひとつしかない。
—パルメニデスが言っていたようなものかな。
—必ずしもそうとは限らない。
—そうか。
—その仮説を考えてみよう。
—了解。
—そうすれば君は問題がもっと単純になると思ってるんだね!
(6)
—さしあたり … それは僕にもわからない。
— うーむ、君が知りたいなら言うけれど、さっきも言ったけど、僕も同じで、まったくわからないという確信がある。
—そうか。
—なるほど。

★ ★ ★

— もしひとつしかなかったとしたらね。しかし君にもわかるだろうが、ほんとうにひとつだけなんだ。
(7)— この馬鹿め!
—なんだって?
—なぜ君は彼にそんなことを言うのかね?

— だって … 忘れてくれ … いや、ほんとうに耐えられないんだ。
— なぜなのか話してくれ！
— まあ、そんなふうに進めなくてもいいじゃないか。尊重すべきは、やはり対話の価値だ。そうでなければ、話がどこにも進まない。
— 聞け、爺さん、しっかりしろ！
(8)— 君は僕にたいして、病人に向かって話すような口の利き方をするね。
— そういうつもりじゃないけれど、君が思うとおりだろう。さあ、僕もしっかりしよう。さっき君は、もっと複雑になるかもしれないと言ってたね … 覚えているかい？
— それが問題なわけじゃない。
— でも、君は複雑性のパルメニデス的な閾値について話してたね。
— そんなことはないよ！。
— もちろん、君が話したことそのままではないのはわかってる [10(原文ママ、9はなし]。でも、すこし話がそういう方向に向いてたんだよ。
— まあ、あなたがそう望むなら！
— いや、たいしたことじゃないから別にいいんだ。
— 僕は興味あるな。続けてくれ。
— つまり、彼はあなたに、それは私たちの関心を牽くだろうと言ったんだ。
— 君たち二人ともいいかげんにしてくれ。
— はっきり言えば、君は僕のことをよく理解していないせいで、僕の話を間違って受け取ったんだな。
— え？

― 君の言葉について(11)僕がわからないって言ったときだ。
― ああ、ひとつしかないっていう話か。
― そう、まさにそれだ。
― そんな怖い顔しないでくれ、僕たちが頑張っているのがわかるだろう?
― そんなこと気にするな!それに君はさっきから話を遮ってばかりいるぞ。
― 僕は彼の話を遮ってるんだ!君は自分の言っていることがわからないのか?
― どうしたんだい?
― どうやら彼は、矛盾というか(12)言葉の転用があると言いたいようだ…。
― そんなのたいしたことじゃない。
― 重要なのはそれじゃない。要はひとつしかなかったとしたら、それを誰が知っているのかってことだ。
― そう!古くからある問題だ…。

＊＊＊

― でも、そこから出発して探すのは…。
― くちばしでつつくもの。
― あるいは尻尾の下に隠すもの。
(13)― いずれ君たちにも僕が言ったことがわかるよ。

＊＊＊

(ユノの登場)
― やあユノ!
― ちゃんと「こんにちわ」って言ったらどうなのよ!
― 僕たちは[原文ママ]話をしていたところなんだ。

— あなたたち、よく飽きないわね。
(彼女は舞台の奥を向き、観客に背中側を見せながら、彼らの前に座る)
ユノ:私のお尻の謎よ。何かあるわ!さあいらっしゃい、私とヤリましょうよ!嫌なわけないでしょうね!
(14)(男たちは同時に肩をすくめる)
— 嫌なわけないね!
まあ、でも遠慮しておく。こういう状況だし。
(彼女は出口のドアを半ば開く)
— 私を買う人はいないの?
(Bが疲れた表情でわずかに手を上げる)
— ひとりいるなら、その人の金タマを撫でてあげて、たくさん可愛がってあげるのに。ほんとうに嫌なの?
(15)
— A:君が何を証明したいのかわからないよ!
[—]BとC:しーっ。彼女にかまうな。
— A:いや冗談抜きで、僕は彼女とヤリたいぞ。
— BとC:しーっ。相手するな。
— ナレーション:雌鶏に答えてはいけない。
(了)

5

German

Translated by Iloe Ariss

(1) Parmenides

— So eine Ansammlung. Ich weiß nicht, Dinge, Menschen, Andenken, es ist kompliziert genug geworden.
— Wegen der Menschen und all der Dinge?
— Ja, wegen denen. Aber auch für alle übrigen.
— Aber was?
— Ach! Ich, ich weiß nicht.

....

— Dann ist er eingetreten, und hat gesagt, "Bewegt ihr nicht!" Eigentlich haben wir uns lange nicht bewogen.
— Und war's schön?
— Du sprichst über ein Ereignis! (2) Ich weiß nun nicht wo ich war
— Du sagtest …
— Ja, ich sagte, dass es kompliziert war.

— Ja, mit den Menschen und allen übrigen.
— Ja, das ist's.
— Und also?

....

— Na ja!
— Wenn es mindestens weniger gäbe.
— Ich weiß nicht, ob das etwas ändern würde.
— Ach!

(3)— Warum sagst du das?
— Es ist durch meinen Kopf gegangen. Achte nicht darauf.
— Nein, es ist normal! Du hast das Recht zu denken, was du denkst.
— Denn ich dir gesagt habe, dass ich es gesagt habe, ohne zu suchen
— Ich möchte mich nicht in ihrem Gespräch einmischen
— In Ordnung.
— Na dann …
— Wir können uns auch überlegen …
— Gut!

(4)— Komm schon, Alter, wir waren dort zum Reden.
— Es geht um die Frage des Wenigens[1]
— Des was?
— Die Tatsache, dass wenn es weniger gäbe vielleicht
— Na ja, vielleicht würden wir nicht wieder finden
— Auf eine Weise …
— Dann …
— Es ist nicht klar

(5)— Na gut.

....

— Schau mal. Es wäre nicht mehr als eine Sache und ein einzelnes Ding, damit die Sache anzugucken
— Ein Ding des Genres Parmenides'
— Nicht unbedingt
— Ja, also …
— Nehmen Sie diese Hypothese an.
— Gerne.
— Also, du glaubst, dass es einfacher wäre!
(6)— A priori … weiß ich nicht.
— Na gut … ich sag's dir. Na gut, doch nicht, meine Meinung nach, wenn du wissen möchtest, ich bin mir sicher, dass es keineswegs einfacher wäre
— Komm schon!
— Gut!

....

— Und, wenn es nur ein Ding gäbe. Aber, schau mal, wirklich nur das eine!
(7)— Armer Kerl!
— Was?
— Ich habe "armer Kerl" gesagt
— Wieso sagst du das?
— Weil … lass es doch … Nein wirklich, ich kann das nicht ertragen—

— Nun was! Sprich.

— Endlich funktioniert es nicht so. Es gibt ebenso die Werte des Dialogs zu achten—also wo, wohin gehen wir?

— Höre gut zu, Alter! Geh weiter!

(8)— Du sprichst mich an, als ob ich ein Kranker wäre.

— Keineswegs, aber du weißt schon, wer er ist. Los, ich versuche weiterzugehen, du hast gerade gesagt, dass es vielleicht komplizierter werden könnte … du erinnerst dich daran …

— Das ist nicht die Frage.

— Doch, du hast von Parmenides' Schwelle der Komplexität gesprochen

— Das ist doch der Gipfel!

— Ja, ich weiß schon, dass das nicht ist, (10) was du gesagt hast. Aber es geht mal in diesem Sinn

— Wenn du das glaubst!

— Aber nein, macht nichts.

— Na los, ich interessiere mich dafür.

— Bis er uns sagt, dass es uns interessiert

— Ihr macht mit mir herum, ihr beide

— Es scheint mir, offen gesagt, dass du das in den falschen Hals gekriegt hast, weil du mich nicht ganz verstanden hast

— Ach?

— Wenn ich gesagt habe, dass ich nicht mehr etwas bin (11) in Bezug auf dein Ding.

— Ja, inwiefern es nur [] als ein Ding gibt

— Das ist's, genau, das ist's!

— Mach dies Gesicht nicht! Du weißt, dass wir versuchen, gut herauszukommen

— Beschäftige dich nicht damit! Und ebenso, du hörst nicht auf zu unterbrechen.
— Ich höre nicht auf zu unterbrechen! Du hörst nicht was du sagst
— Was ist los?
— Er meint, dass es eine Art von Widerspruch (12) gibt, eine Art von Katachrese
— Das hat nichts damit zu tun.
— Egal, das Ding ist, wenn es nur ein Ding gäbe, wäre niemand dabei, um das zu wissen usw …
— Ach ja! Das ist ein altes Ding …

....

— Und wenn wir von dort ausgehen, um zu finden …
— Etwas zu knabbern
— Wir müssen uns in die Schlange stellen (in den Krieg eintreten?) (13)— Endlich greift ihr, was ich sage?

....

Juno tritt ein.
— Hi Juno!
— Du könntest mal Hallo sagen!
— Haben wir eben gesagt
— Ihr ermüdet nicht
Sie setzt sich den zwei gegenüber, Rücken zum Publikum.
— Das Rätsel meines Pos! Ist doch nichts! Komm, meine Schöne, fick mich. Ist es nicht schrecklich?
(14) Die drei zucken gleichzeitig mit den Schultern.
— Ist es nicht schrecklich!
— Na gut! Nichts. Es ist so

Sie öffnet ihren Käfig.

— Möchte jemand?

B ~~Er hebt,~~ erhebt leicht seine Hand, überdrüssig anscheinend

— Und wenn ich [] ein [hätte]! Wenn ich sich meine Hand zwischen die   Hoden_____

Wenn ich mich durchdrehe_____ein bisschen überall_____nein wirklich_____?

(15) A: Wir sehen nicht, was du demonstrieren willst_____!

B und C: Sch!_____ ... Lass es.

— A: aber nein, kein Scherz. Ich will sie ficken ___ ___ ___

B und C: sch! Lass es dabei ___ ___ ___

Eine Stimme: Antworten Sie nicht darauf?????? ____

Dem Manuskript fehlt die neunte Seite, aber dieser Mangel stört die Verständlichkeit des Textes nicht.

Note

1   As opposed to "die Frage der Wenigen" the question of the few. i.e., the privileging of few over many. I went with singular "Wenigen" to mean the concept of "moins" or "less."

6

Polish

Translated by Benjamin Bandosz

(1) Parmenides

— Tyle tej akumulacji. Nie znam rzeczy, wspomnień ludzi … Zrobiło się to skomplikowane.

— Przez ludzi i rzeczy?

— Tak, przez nich, ale i może przez wszytko.

— Ale co?

— Oj! Naprawdę nie wiem.

✳ ✳ ✳

— No wszedł, i powiedział: nie ruszaj się więcej! A faktycznie już nie ruszaliśmy się od dawna.

— I to było w porządku?

— Mówisz o zdarzeniu! (2) Już nie wiem gdzie byłem.

— Mówiłeś …

— Tak mówiłem, że było skomplikowane

— Tak, z ludźmi i wszystkim innym.

— Tak jest.

— Cóż
— No tak!

* * *

— Gdyby chociaż było mniej tego wszystkiego.
— Nie jestem pewny, żeby to coś zmieniło.
— Oj!

(3) — Czemu to powiedziałeś?
— Przyszło mi do głowy. Nie przejmuj się.
— Co tam, to normalne. Masz prawo, żeby myśleć, co chcesz.
— Skoro Ci powiedziałem, że powiedziałem to, bez zastanowienia.
— Nie chciałbym się wtrącać w Waszą rozmowę.
— Dobra.
— No i co …
— Możemy także wziąć pod uwagę …
— Okej

(4) — Dawaj stary, przyszliśmy tu, żeby pogadać.
— To jest kwestia tego, czego jest mniej.
— Czego?
— Faktu, że jeśli byłoby mniej
— No i może tam nie znajdziemy się już więcej
— W pewnym sensie …
— A więc!
— To nie jest oczywiste
(5) — No dobra

* * *

— Słuchaj. Byłoby tylko jedna rzecz i jeden sposób, żeby ująć tą rzecz
— Coś w stylu Parmenidesa
— Nie do końca.
— No i cóż
— Weź pod uwagę tą hipotezę
— Zgoda
— Więc, wierzysz, że to byłoby prostsze
(6)— A priori … Nie wiem
— No … To Ci zaraz powiem. No dobra, nie wcale nie, po mojemu, jeśli chcesz wiedzieć, jestem sam pewny, że w ogóle nic nie ma.
— Serio!
— Dobra!

* * *

— I jeśli było tylko tą jedyną rzeczą. Ale, widzisz, naprawdę tylko jedna!
(7)— Biedny sukinsyn!
— Co takiego?
— Powiedziałem, biedny sukinsyn
— Czemu to powiedziałeś?
— Bo … nie, daj spokój … Nie, naprawdę, nie znoszę tego—
— No co! Mów
— Faktycznie, to nie działa w taki sposób. Jest i etyka rozmowy, którą trzeba przestrzegać. Dokąd teraz idziemy?

— Słuchaj, stary, spróbuj się pozbierać!
(8)— Gadasz do mnie, jakbym był psycholem.
— Wcale nie, ale dobrze widzisz co jest. No dobra, spróbuję się zorientować … Mówiłeś, że to może będzie bardziej skomplikowane. Pamiętasz?

— Nie chodzi o to

— Ale tak, przedtem gadałeś o progu Parmenidesa złożoności.

— Daj spokój!

— Dobrze wiem, to nie jest (10) to, co ty powiedziałeś. To właśnie szło w tym kierunku.

— Jeśli tak twierdzisz!

— Nie, ach, to nie ma znaczenia

— No dawaj, zaintrygowałeś mnie

— Zaraz powie, że to nas interesuje

— Wy dwaj mnie wkurwiacie.

— Wydaje mi się, szczerze mówiąc, że źle przyjąłeś to co powiedziałem, bo mnie nie zrozumiałeś za dobrze.

— Tak?

— Kiedy powiedziałem, że już nie czaję (11) o co chodzi z twoją rzeczą

— Tak, jakby chodziło mi tylko o jedną rzecz.

— Dokładnie, tak właśnie jest.

— Nie rób tej gęby, dobrze wiesz, że próbujemy iść naprzód

— Nie martw się! I po pierwsze, ciągle mi przerywasz

— Nie przystanę przerywać! Nie słyszysz tego, co sam mówisz

— Co ci jest?

— Chcę powiedzieć, że jest pewien rodzaj sprzeczności, (12) rodzaj katachrezy

— To nie ma z tym nic wspólnego

— Nie ma znaczenia, rzecz w tym, że gdyby była tylko jedna, nikt by tego nie wiedział.

— No tak! To odwieczny problem

* * *

— Nawet zaczynając od tego, żeby znaleźć ...
— Jakąś przekąskę
— Musimy wrócić na swoje miejsce.
(13)— Wreszcie, widzicie to co chcę powiedzieć?

✳ ✳ ✳

Wejście Juno
— Cześć Juno!
— Mógłbyś powiedzieć dzień dobry!
— Przecież przywitaliśmy się
— Nie przejmuj się
Siada przeciwko nim, plecami do widzów
— Tajemnica mojej dupy. To dopiero coś, nie?! Dawaj, mój przystojniaku, zerżnij mnie! Ale zajebiste, nie?!
(14) Wszyscy trzej wzruszają ramionami
— Ale zajebiste!
     Dobra. Nic. Czasami tak jest.
Ona otwiera swój welon
— Są jacyś chętni?
B powoli podnosi rękę
— I jeśli mam jednego? Włożę rękę między jego jaja. Jeśli pomieszam tu i tam, nie naprawdę?
(15)— A: Nie widzimy co chcesz pokazać!
B i C: Sza ... zostaw to
— A: Ale nie, bez żartów. Chcę ją pieprzyć!
B i C: Sza! Zostaw to już
Głos poza sceną: Nie odpowiadaj ...

Acknowledgement

I would like to thank Agnieszka Jeżyk for her comments and insights on my translation.

7

Russian

Translated by Mikhail Fedorchenko

(1) Парменид

— Всё это напряжение … Я даже не знаю …, от вещей, от воспоминаний о людях … всё стало каким— то сложным.

— Из— за людей и вещей[1]?

— Да, из— за них, но и из— за всего остального тоже.

— Но из— за чего?

— О! Да я и сам не знаю.

✶✶✶

— Потом он вошёл и сказал: «Море волнуется раз!».[2] Хотя на самом деле, мы давно уже не двигались.

— И всё прошло хорошо?

— Да это было такое событие! (2) Так, я что— то потерял нить повествования.

— Ты говорил …

— Да, я говорил, что это было сложно.

— Да, насчёт людей и всего остального.

— Это верно.

— Так что.

— Ну, да!

✱✱✱

— Если хотя бы было меньше …

— Я не уверен, что это что— то изменит.

— Ах!

— (3) Зачем ты это сказал?

— Да просто в голову пришло. Не обращай внимания.

— Нет, это нормально! Ты имеешь право думать то, что думаешь.

— Раз уж я говорю вам, что просто брякнул[3] первое что в голову пришло.

— Я бы не хотел вмешиваться в ваш разговор …

— Понятно.

— Ну, хорошо.

— Можно также подумать …

— Окей.

— (4) Продолжай, приятель, мы тут болтаем.

— Это про то, что неплохо бы меньше.

— А именно?

— О том, что если бы, возможно, их было меньше …

— Да, возможно, нам тогда бы не пришлось иметь дело ни с чем больше …

— В каком-то смысле …

— В таком случае!

— Это не точно.
— (5) О, хорошо.

***

— Ты вот подумай. Существовала бы только одна вещь[4] и только один способ рассмотреть её.
— Парменидова штука.[5]
— Не обязательно.
— Ну, и потом.
— Давай рассмотрим эту гипотезу.
— Прекрасно.
— Итак, ты считаешь, что так было бы проще!
(6)— Априори, я не знаю.
— Ну … Вот что вам скажу. Ну, нет, на мой взгляд, и если хочешь знать, я даже

уверен, что совсем нет.
— Правда!
— Хорошо!

***

— И если бы существовала лишь одна вещь. Но взаправду лишь только одна!
— (7) Бедняга!
— Что?
— Я сказал «бедняга».
— Почему ты так сказал?
— Потому что … неважно … Нет, правда, я не могу вынести …
— Ну, что! Говори.

— Ну, так не пойдет. Ценности диалога все еще нужно уважать.— Иначе,
куда мы пойдем дальше?
— Слушай, приятель, возьми себя в руки!
— (8) Ты говоришь со мной, как с больным.
— Вовсе нет, но ты понимаешь, о чем идет речь. Давай я попробую начать сначала. Ты сказал, что это было сложно. Ты помнишь …
— Вопрос не в этом.
— Как раз таки в этом, ты говорил о парменидовском пороге сложности.
— Это уже последняя капля!
— Я знаю, что это не то (10), что ты сказали. Но мысль шла в эту сторону.
— Как скажешь!
— Нет, ну это неважно.
— Продолжай, теперь мне интересно.
— Потом он скажет, что это нас интересует.
— Вы оба меня бесите.
— Честно говоря, мне кажется, что ты воспринял мои слова неправильно, потому что не смог понять меня.
— О?
— Когда я сказал, что больше (11) не понимаю, что ты говоришь о своей штуке.
— Да, как будто существует только одна вещь.
— Именно так. Именно так.
— Не дуйся, ты же видишь, что мы пытаемся двигаться вперед.
— Не волнуйся! И потом, ты продолжаешь перебивать.

— Я не могу перестать перебивать. Ты не слышишь, что говоришь.

— В чем дело?

— Он имеет в виду, что существует некое противоречие (12), своего рода катахреза[6]…

— Это не имеет никакого отношения к делу.

— Неважно, дело в том, что если бы существовало только одно, то не было бы никого, кто бы его осознавал, и т. д.

— Ах, да, это древний вопрос[7]…

***

— Даже начиная отсюда, чтобы найти …

— На что— нибудь опереться.

— Мы должны вернуться в строй …

(13)— Ну, теперь вы понимаете, о чем я?

***

Входит Юнона.

— Привет, Юнона!

— Ты могла бы сказать «привет».

— А мы тут так, болтаем ….

— Поберегите дыхание.

Она садится лицом к ним, спиной к зрителям.

— Тайна моих ягодиц. Это что-то! Давай, детка, трахни меня![8] Разве это не ужасно, не правда ли!

(14) Все трое вместе пожимают плечами.

— Это ужасно, не так ли!

Не правда ли! Ничего страшного. Просто так получилось.

Она открывает клетку.

— Есть желающие?

Б слегка поднимает руку с усталым видом.

— А что если..? Если я просуну руку между его яйцами. Если я засуну её себе. Ну как?

(14)— А. Мы не видим, что ты там показываешь!

— Б и В: Цыц … оставь ее в покое.

— А: без шуток. Я хочу ее трахнуть.

— Б и В: Цыц, оставь ее в покое.

Голос из— за кулис. Не отвечайте …

Notes

1 Количество и личности персонажей не уточняются, как и порядок их участия (кроме Юноны в конце)

2 Можно перевести и в контексте детской игры «море волнуется раз!»: «замрите», «стоп» и тп.

3 В оригинале «сказал без усилий»

4 Truc во французском это и «вещь», и «трюк», ии «вопрос». В тексте неоднократно это обыгрывается

5 «Бытие одно, и не может быть двух и более «бытий». Иначе они должны были бы быть отграничены друг от друга— Небытием»

6 Троп или стилистическая ошибка, неправильное или необычное употребление сочетаний слов с несовместимыми буквальными лексическими значениями

7 Truc

8 Во франзузском un baiser означает «поцелуй», но как глагол baiser означает «трахать», так что Baise-moi означает «Трахни меня». Интересно созвучно с романом и фильмом Вирджини Депант «Baise-moi»

PART TWO
COMMENTARIES

8
From Logic to Rhythm

Gary Genosko

Guattari's *Parmenides* partakes in a little Platonic humor by joining those who would cast aspersions on Parmenides' thesis that all is one, a position exposed early on in Plato's *Parmenides*, by showing that his supposition—there is but one—results in "absurdities and contradictions" (*Parm.* 128d).[1] It is the disciple Zeno, in Plato's dialog, who comes to the defense of his teacher Parmenides, in the recitation of the encounter of Zeno and Parmenides and a young Socrates by Antiphon. "Against plurality"—that is, the point of Zeno's defense, because support for plurality leads to even greater absurdities than the hypothesis of the one (meaning merely, not many). Socrates recasts the argument in terms of the theory of the forms, with a few odd restrictions thrown in (there is no form for mud, 130c). Below, we will see how Alain Badiou casts himself as the anti-Zeno in the name of multiplicity.

In the meantime, the figure of Parmenides offers a master class in the weaknesses of the theory of forms, but this is not Félix's direct inspiration. It is, rather, the theory of the one that is set upon, which is what Parmenides is convinced to defend, perhaps against his better judgment (*Parm.* 137). What he does is enumerate, page after page, the one's negative attributes—what it is not, what it cannot do. Until he reaches the self-erasing principle: "the one in no sense *is* ... the one neither is one nor is at all" (141e–142). Upon reconsideration of the negations, Parmenides rebuilds the positive implications of the one having being (and, not incidentally, not-being as well, 162b), which turns out to imply that the one is many (145a); except if there is no one, and only things other than it, and since they cannot be one, and are no-thing, that is, not many: neither one nor many. Finally, the fictionalized Parmenides concludes his puzzling presentation: "if there is no one, there is nothing at all" (166b).

Famously, Deleuze and Guattari in *A Thousand Plateaus* call the "magic formula we all seek" the strange equation: pluralism = monism.[2] In his *Parmenides*, Guattari is trying out a process, the very process that he and Deleuze invoked that would go through (pass via them) dualisms in order to challenge all such models based upon them. The challenge of ontological dualism built around the one and many by the equals sign, indicating equality, is that the process is never finished, and does not, as the authors claim, give rise to another type of dualism.

Another seeker points us in a different direction. Badiou, in pursuit of how to subtract being from the one, reminds us of Socrates' introduction of difference as a kind of "otherness" in *Parmenides* (143b) and in the *Sophist* (258c-d),[3] against Parmenides' injunction against asserting the being of what is not. The demonstration based on difference and not self-sameness yields a big "O"-type Otherness: "the multiple's immanent alterity gives rise to a process of limitless self-differentiation" and that if the multiple is not, there is not one, but nothing (no concession—there are only multiples of multiples). This is the "pure inconsistent multiplicity"[4] that resists definition and explanation and designation, and consists only of multiples, never ones. Badiou translated Plato's "affirmation" of the "positivity of difference"[5] into "multiple without oneness," which is designed to "discontinue" the power of the one in the name of ontology turned into mathematics (axiomatic set theory), what Daniel Smith rightly calls "reductionist,"[6] setting up a conflict between a *major mathematics* and a *minor problematics*, Badiou or Deleuze. However, we need to rein in this analysis and refocus first on what Badiou does to Parmenides, and then on why Guattari resists this in his theatrical piece.

Guattari found Plato's aggravating dialog of building-up and -down fertile ground for his theatrical experiment. The contradiction that emerges is the dramatic focus: the "less" is "more." Yet Guattari turns it into a semio-epistemological drama, not so much a strictly ontological one, which suggests how seriously one should take the "Parmenides-type" issue, by slipping in the philosopher himself, the subject of the statement, but as a shifter that doesn't confirm his existence at all, in fact, it is not Parmenides who speaks in Plato's dialog, but Antiphon. Still, there is some avoiding the obvious at play here as the philosophical reference point both is and is not Parmenides—"not necessarily" him, it, whatever, a fiction of Plato to be sure. Nonetheless, it would be appropriate to recall Plato's praise of Parmenides in the *Theaetetus*, where Socrates refers to him as "reverend and awful" (*Theaet.* 183e), possessed of a "noble depth," at least in the eyes of a young man looking upon a revered elder.[7]

There is also a hint of indecision between contradiction and catachresis. Of course, they are not the same, the first indicating what would become known as the Aristotelian law of non-contradiction that a thing cannot be at once and in the same respect what it is and what it is not. Whereas catachresis is an incorrect usage of a term that breaks a rule, that is, to speak about the one thing is to add to it, to make it plural, if only in the epistemological version in which the subject is implied. But in the case of semantic misuse, someone doing the misusing is implied. Perhaps we can look at the challenge in translating *truc* as a good example. It is not simply a thing, but more than that, it is the one thing, but also a long-standing philosophical preoccupation of the ancients, less a ruse than an acknowledgment of historical depth and logical convolution, the latter typical of the Eleatics, especially Zeno with his love of paradox. Yet it is also a word with multiple meanings, always more than less, until one settles on some meaning. The fundamental plurality of language is constantly re-asserting itself within the context of the difficulty of dialog and the tenuousness of meaning. Indeed, if everything was really one, one speaker, one meaning, would there be any meaning at all? Doesn't plurality alone commit one to respect for "the values of dialog"? Oneness means silence.

And as for a certain Juno, name of the Roman deity of women, who is certainly not shy about exposing herself to the assembled. Even though the goddess had many guises and symbols, this Juno is not typically one of them. What Guattari was aiming at here is lost in the limitations of the surviving fragment. What a woman named for a matron goddess is doing humiliating a trio of philosophers is anyone's guess. They are certainly low-hanging fruit and not very priapic, as we find out, in a blending of impotence and desire. It is most likely that Guattari was working on a pastiche of Parmenides' "*Poem*,"[8] in which mention is made of a similar goddess, perhaps Aphrodite, and the mischievous "son," Eros. In fact, there are many goddesses hinted at in the stanzas, though not named. Indeed, many of the fragments concerning sexual intercourse may be spurious; some translations do not include them (for an exception, see below, n. 17). The welcome the poet receives by the maidens of Justice (Dike or Themis?) upon passing through the gates of night and day and heading off on a cosmic journey is only an oneiric entry into her "mysteries," if Guattari's play on dream interpretation can be accepted. We remain cognizant of Martin Heidegger's insistence on translating truth as "unconcealedness," a concealedness taken away, pulled back, a *cage* opened or exposed in the sense of a rebuff?[9] The philosophers must remain on the verge of getting it on. The text ends abruptly. They are broken off, or rejected like a suitor. Whatever is opened slightly suggests a refusal as much as an offer.

It may be productive to briefly consider Luce Irigaray's remark about how Parmenides, separated by her from other pre-Socratics with regard to his attitude toward nature, "still alludes to what they receive from her—nature, woman, Goddess—and their discourse still assumes the form of poems in which rhythm and melody take part in the meaning."[10] In short, Parmenides writes in what is considered a poem or proem and thus remains close to feminine vibrations from which meaning is not separated or extracted and applied in various masculinist techniques (logic, philosophy) and differentiations (dichotomies, dualisms). In Guattari's *Parmenides* a goddess suddenly manifests and inserts herself into the proceedings, maintaining the

Parmenidean connection to mother/nature. This is how Guattari stays close to both Plato (dialog) and Parmenides (p[r]oem), in principle.

Indeed, returning to Badiou and Parmenides, we see in the former's separation of poetry from philosophy the use of the latter's "Poem" in a specific manner: it is "*not yet* philosophy."[11] Yet Parmenides is given some credit for providing a "pre-moment" that interrupts the poetic-sacred narrative by the secular-argumentation of reasoning in a "depoeticization." When Guattari retains the goddess, although a later one, he nonetheless repoeticizes what is a quarrel in a Platonic dialog and opens the way for the shift from logic to rhythm. The appearance of Juno in the most broken segment of Guattari's text dramatizes the act of philosophy's exposure to poetry in the opening of her *cage*, with deference to Badiou. But any resistance to exclusion and the boxing out of poetry which would arrive with Plato is forestalled by Guattari's use of the philosophical dramatization as the double effect of poetry on philosophy: it at once conditions and insults it, as Badiou would have it.[12]

Guattari's theatrical dialog engages in talk about talking, if you will, at one point even urging: "Come on pal, we're here to talk." And at other moments extolling or demanding the "values of dialog" which should be "respected" by all interlocutors. Theatrical and not Socratic dialog: a dialog that is not only a demonstration of argumentative prowess but of intersubjective interactions, anticipations, interruptions, and idioms ("Get hold of yourself!")! The rhythms of speech are front and center in Guattari's dialog, and it may be said to concern itself with them to the extent that they hold aloft and carry forward the progression, especially in the face of digressions and putting words into another's mouth ("I'm aware that it's not what you said. But it was going in that direction") of the demonstration of the instability of Parmenidean monism. The stakes of oneness are in fact revealed through interruption and misrecognition. Crossing the so-called Parmenidean threshold of complexity into a myriad of mis-memory ("Remember ... you had spoken of ... give me a break!") brings an almost accidental insight: could it be the thing that you were going on about is the "single" thing that cannot be "less" than it is: "Yes, as if there was merely a single thing. / That's it. That is exactly it." But this is what was almost lost in the exchange, "When I said I no longer follow what you were saying about your thing (*truc*)." Perhaps this is just as easily translated as "formula": being is one.

Is this, then, part of what is meant by the much-vaunted yet "puzzling" *philo-performance*?[13] The "staging of thought" in a dialog shot through with all of the beats of everyday dialog, including interruptions, disagreements, and misunderstandings, yet indexed to an ancient metaphysical conundrum? That is only revealed in its complexity, stepping over the aforementioned threshold, when it is subject to a subtraction of the knower: "the thing is that if there was only one, there would not be anyone to know it, etc." And, yet, why can't the one contain this contrary property? Maybe subtraction is meaningless if humans could not know the one, anyway, or if the knower and what is known are incompatible. This is "an ancient issue" (the unity of thinking and being) to be sure, but it also stages thought's convoluted pathways along the logical problems that arise in addressing the one.

But if the emphasis in a rhythm exercise is on vibrations, fecundity, and becoming, surely the knots of meaning cannot be separated out, and the figure of Juno underwrites this, especially her connection with mothering, which holds together the connection between vibrations and meaning so that they cannot be torn asunder. Isn't this vibrational domain akin to the infra-quark universe that Guattari explores through his screenplay *A Love of UIQ*?[14] A universe that knows no oppositions, binaries, or dichotomies, a dispersed field of desire and cosmic subjectivity—"whose particles are constructed from galaxies"[15]—and its temporary machinic actualizations. UIQ consists of vibrating particles at an elementary scale—"a cognitivity constituted on the scale of quarks"[16]—in this science-fictional scenario of an abstract extraterrestrial. UIQ's violence, its regression to childhood jealousy and eventual attachment to binaries of all sorts, is ultimately realized as it betrays the female protagonist Janice, even denying her the relief of death, forcing her to survive tremendous violence. The vibrations do not stop, they force others to endure, an insistent and cruel masculinist misapplication of a feminine principle.

"You talk to me like I'm ill/Not at all, but you can see what the point is": is this a recrimination for a woolly schizosophy with pretensions to classical status? As a writer, to put it in a Barthesian way, Guattari satirizes the "talking cure" by showing how it is suffused with "tedious labor"—but not as Freud imagined it by making conscious what is unconscious, lifting repression, and filling in memory gaps in the analysand's accounts, all of which need to be communicated. Interpret, discover, communicate. Recall it was Breuer's patient's (Anna O.) coinage. When it comes to recriminations, talking gains another kind of traction besides catharsis: the analysand says to the analyst: "[Y]ou talk to me like I'm ill." A transference gone bad, full of resistance, it could be just a cry for understanding: "It seems to me, frankly, that you have taken what I said the wrong way … ".

Dynamic miscommunication is woven into the problem of the logical inconsistencies of Parmenidean Monism, as it is in psychoanalysis. The analyst doesn't have much to say ("Talk to me about Parmenides, is he your philosophical daddy?"), after all, as it is the analysand's role to produce discourse and make accusations ("Oh, not more ancient history"!).

What is the point of reaching or achieving philosophy, of passing into it, then, from something earlier? Both the ancient "Poem," and the modern theatrical dialog surely forestall a complete passage into philosophical logic by retaining elements of the rhythmical-feminine, following Irigaray. After all, it is the unnamed goddess who speaks the truths of a poem. Readers of Parmenides' "Poem" like Fernando Santoro are attuned to the cosmic-erotic dimension of a universe as a desiring-machine, and the mutuality of masculine-feminine forces is exemplified in the tangled limbs of copulating lovers in a contested fragment.[17] We are reminded, however, of certain translators of Parmenides' "Poem," such as Stanley Lombardo,[18] who adopt a psychedelic approach and interiorize the sprawling mythic landscape of the voyage thus described. A sort of "shamanism" highlights the encounter with pure Being that ends not, perhaps, in a hosted orgy, but in an observed act of procreation that would not be out of place alongside Antonioni's lusty hippies in *Zabriskie Point*!

What is at issue in rhythm is more, then, than mere pacing. Show respect for the melody of the text and the passage of time. For what is not yet masculine is processual, becoming. The patriarchical one has its precursor, and perhaps its postcursor as well, in the two, or many more. It is rhythm that keeps us unglued from logic and keeps us moving from logic to rhythm and back again, establishing connections, keeping in touch, staying in passage, between worlds, bodies, and characters. The gap between characters is an anti-one. In this generative interval, the middle of becoming, Guattari's decision to slip out of the clutches of Parmenidean Monism affirms the insight of Flore Garcin-Marrou about the Dadaist character of this dialog. For we remember what psychoanalyst Richard Huelsenbeck affirmed: "The Dadaist sides with Heraclitus against Parmenides."[19]

Madness haunts Guattari's early philosophers. This is the characterization of Georges, who believes himself to be Socrates. Mr. and Mrs. Socrates, the Socrateses, Georges and Carmen, are taking delivery of a parcel by a disgraced postman, and Georges is struggling to open it. His adversary, Challenger, Carmen's lover, a notable figure from *A Thousand Plateaus*, completes the trio. As Garcin-Marrou tells us, *Socrates* was the only play of Guattari's to be performed.[20] Georges is trapped in delirium, and this turns Socrates into a ridiculous figure, mocked by children as "Father Hemlock." The inspiration is clearly Aristophanes' *Clouds*, for his Socrates was a pompous aerial acrobat of sophistic argumentation, and Challenger, a professor of below, the earth; Guattari's Socrates is, too, a sophistic schizo, with a penchant for pointing at the sky looking for American military airplanes (eventually an American parachutist comes through the ceiling). Nevertheless, there are traces of Plato's *Phaedo* in Guattari's text, especially Georges' bulging eyes', just like Socrates' "favorite trick" of opening his eyes really wide![21]

Yet Georges' struggle is with a parcel. This theater of delivery does not go as far as obstruction of correspondence, but is simply a failure to open by the addressee, rather than opening somebody else's mail. Guattari puts the emphasis on the receiver, and we never learn anything about the sender, but for the "foreign stamp" and perhaps a place, New Delhi, Delphi? It could be from India, it could be from Greece, who knows! Georges can neither open the parcel nor open himself to Carmen, despite her repeated urging. It is not to Freud's Little Hans that we should look but, instead, to Clever Hans. Stuck with the destination, we should look sideways at Thomas Sebeok's famous dictum: "looking in the destination for what should have been sought in the source." Deprived of the source, we are condemned to the destination in which looking is also not much of an option as the parcel is never opened. It is signed for but has no signified. In remaining sealed, un-opened, a time capsule, the parcel takes on a different role: perhaps as a MacGuffin, that pretext that moves the dialog along but is elusive, its content is absent. In the end, the parcel, abandoned by Georges, is seized by the feet of the hanging Challenger, dressed as an American soldier, who slowly lifts off through the ceiling, as Georges desperately clings to his legs. The contrast with *Parmenides* could not be starker, if we recall the figure of Juno, who opens her basket, although what is revealed is not clear; she is the goddess of new lunar cycles, and of monthly menstrual cycles. Socrates is the anti-opening, non-cyclical, poor keeper of a closed text. We might recall the difference between the receiver and the destination in the Shannon-Weaver model, the so-called postal service model, since Challenger turns out to be the default destination of the still unopened parcel. We can look all we want, but there is nothing to see in this destination, either. It simply beats a path through the dialog. Yet it is not a feeble guess to claim that it might contain hemlock, as Guattari transposes the cup from which Socrates drank in Plato's account in the *Phaedo*[22] to the parcel that

Socrates fails to open. It is not hard to imagine a prepared poison hemlock drink made for home delivery.

Notes

1 Plato, "Parmenides," in *The Collected Dialogues*, trans. F. M. Cornford, Princeton, NJ: Princeton University Press, 1961, sn., 126–66.

2 Deleuze and Guattari, *A Thousand Plateaus*, trans. Brian Massumi, Minneapolis, MN: University of Minnesota Press, 1987, 20.

3 Plato, *Sophist*, trans. F. M. Cornford, in *The Collected Dialogues*, sn., 216–68.

4 Alain Badiou, "The Question of Being Today," in *Theoretical Writings*, ed. and trans Ray Brassier and Alberto Toscano, London: Continuum, 2004, 45.

5 Alain Badiou, *Logic of Worlds*, trans. A. Toscano, London: Continuum, 2009, 121.

6 Daniel Smith, "Mathematics and the Theory of Multiplicities," *The Southern Journal of Philosophy* XLI (2003): 412.

7 Plato, *Theaetetus*, trans F. M. Cornford and Benjamin Jowett, in *The Collected Dialogues*, sn., 142–210.

8 *Parmenides of Elea: Fragments*, trans. David Gallop, Toronto: University of Toronto Press, 1984.

9 Martin Heidegger, *Parmenides*, trans. André Schuwer and Richard Rojcewicz, Bloomington, IN: Indiana University Press, 1992, 13–14.

10 Luce Irigaray, "Before and beyond Any Word," in *Key Writings*, London: Continuum, 2004, 136.

11 Badiou, "Philosophy and Art," in *Infinite Thought*, trans. Oliver Feltham and Justin Clemens, London: Continuum, 2003, 92.

12 Ibid., 101.

13 Amalia Boyer, Flore Garcin-Marrou *et alia*, "What Is Philo-Performance: A Roundtable," *Performance Philosophy* 1 (2015): 158, n. 1.

14 Guattari, *A Love of UIQ*, trans. Silvia Maglioni and Graeme Thomson, Minneapolis, MN: Univocal, 2012.

15 Guattari, *Chaosmosis*, trans. Paul Bains, Bloomington, IN: Indiana University, 1995, 52.

16 Ibid.

17 Fernando Santoro, "Venus and the Erotics of Parmenides," *Anais de Filosofia Clàssica* 28 (2020): 176–77.

18 *Parmenides and Empedocles: The Fragments in Verse Translation*, trans. and intro. Stanley Lombardo, San Francisco, CA: Grey Fox, 1979.

19 Richard Huelsenbeck, *Memoirs of a Dadaist Drummer*, ed. H. J. Kleinschmidt, trans. Joachim Neugroschel, New York: Viking Press, 1969, 160.

20 Flore Garcin-Marrou, "To Be or Not to Be Socrates: Introduction to the translation of Félix Guattari's *Socrates*," *Deleuze Studies* 6/2 (2012): 171.

21 Plato, "Phaedo", trans. Hugh Tredennick, in *The Collected Dialogues*, sn., 86d.

22 Plato, "Phaedo", in *The Collected Dialogues*, sn. 117a-b.

References

Badiou, Alain, *Infinite Thought*, trans. Oliver Feltham and Justin Clemens, London: Continuum, 2003.

Badiou, Alain, *Theoretical Writings*, ed. and trans. Ray Brassier and Alberto Toscano, London: Continuum, 2004.

Badiou, Alain, *Logic of Worlds*, trans. Alberto Toscano, London: Continuum, 2009.

Boyer, Amalia, Garcin-Marrou, Flore et alia, "What Is Philo-Performance: A Roundtable," *Performance Philosophy* 1 (2015): 148–60.

Deleuze, Gilles, and Félix Guattari, *A Thousand Plateaus*, trans. Brian Massumi, Minneapolis, MN: University of Minnesota Press, 1987.

Garcin-Marrou, Flore, "To Be or Not to Be Socrates: Introduction to the Translation of Félix Guattari's *Socrates*," *Deleuze Studies* 6/2 (2012): 170–2.

Guattari, Félix, *Chaosmosis*, trans. Paul Bains, Bloomington, IN: Indiana University, 1995.

Guattari, Félix, *A Love of UIQ*, trans. Silvia Maglioni and Graeme Thomson, Minneapolis, MN: Univocal, 2012.

Heidegger, Martin, *Parmenides*, trans. André Schuwer and Richard Rojcewicz, Bloomington, IN: Indiana University Press, 1992.

Huelsenbeck, Richard, *Memoirs of a Dadaist Drummer*, ed. Hans J. Kleinschmidt, trans. Joachim Neugroschel, New York: Viking Press, 1969.
Irigaray, Luce, *Key Writings*, London: Continuum, 2004.
Parmenides, *Parmenides and Empedocles: The Fragments in Verse Translation*, trans. and intro. Stanley Lombardo, San Francisco, CA: Grey Fox, 1979.
Parmenides, *Parmenides of Elea: Fragments*, trans. David Gallop, Toronto: University of Toronto Press, 1984.
Plato, *The Collected Dialogues*, trans. F. M. Cornford, Princeton, NJ: Princeton University Press, 1961.
Santoro, Fernando, "Venus and the Erotics of Parmenides," *Anais de Filosofia Clàssica* 28 (2020): 165–89.
Smith, Daniel, "Mathematics and the Theory of Multiplicities," *The Southern Journal of Philosophy* XLI (2003): 411–49.

9

Being, Oneness and Desire in Guattari's *Parménide*

Carlos A. Segovia

1 / A Tale of Two Registers

"[N]e bougez plus !" The first twelve pages of this brief theatrical dialog (Guattari, *Parménide*, IMEC, GTR 22.11) turn around the anxiety caused by exposure to multiplicity: "*Toute cette accumulation. Je ne sais pas, de choses, de gens de souvenirs ... c'est devenu assez compliqué.*" Nonetheless, they deal too with the difficulty that attempts to transform the Multiple into One—"*Un truc genre Parménide*"— inevitably face: "*Si au moins il y en avait moins*"—"*Je ne suis pas sûr que ça changerait quelque chose.*"[1] Arguably, with this the psychoanalytic register unfolds into a philosophical register where, as in Parmenides, ontology (i.e., the discourse on "being") and henology (i.e., the discourse on being's "oneness") overlap.

2 / Being, Non-being, Oneness, and Manifoldness in Parmenides

Parmenides' tacit way of reasoning (in frags. DK B2, B3, B4, and B8) can be summarized thus:

i   Is "non-being" less *or* more than "being"? Consider the following two sentences: (1) "I am"; (2) "H(omer) is not." The latter sentence ("H is not") *begins* by presupposing H ("H is … ") and it *then* negates it (" … not"). Therefore, it can be affirmed that "non-being" is, from a *logical* standpoint, *more*, not less, than being: "H is not" = (H is) + (not).²

ii Now, what can we deduce from the fact that "non-being" is more than being? That non-being is *unthinkable as such*; for, in order to affirm something's non-being, we must first affirm its being ("H is … not"). This is what Parmenides means to say in frag. DK B2: "Only two ways of search can be thought of: first, that it is and that it cannot not-be—a way of persuasion; second, that it is not and that non-being must be—a way which is untrustworthy."

iii Furthermore, if "non-being" is unthinkable, then, in rigor, only "being" is *thinkable*. Hence, too, Parmenides' frag. DK B3: "being and thought are the same."

iv But then (we transit now from the ontological to the henological) "being" must be *one*, as otherwise there would *be* something *else*, i.e., there would be something *other* than "being," namely, "non-being"—and yet, as we have seen, "non-being" is not. By the same token, "being" must be "uncreated," "indestructible," "complete," "endless," etc., as Parmenides claims in frag. DK B8. Affirming this implies, in turn, that being is also "continuous": it cannot be said that "it was," or that "it will be," but that it is "now, all at once" (as we read, too, in that same fragment). Hence, the metaphor of the "sphere" (which is found in it, as well).[3]

v   Consequently, Parmenides goes on to say in fragment DK B4, *no* single "being" can be "held apart" *from* the ontological oneness comprising (all) being(s).

Does this mean that Parmenides denied—as is commonly but wrongly assumed—being's inherent *multiplicity* (for being may be one in one sense, as Parmenides contends; yet it is certainly manifold, i.e., there are, perceptibly, different types of beings and countable beings)? The fact that, before Plato and within the Eleatic school, to affirm (i.e., to predicate) something (B) of something else (A)—as in: A *is* B—amounted to designating the subject's identity, and hence *its being*,[4] bespeaks otherwise, for one can predicate different qualities of a single subject.

3 / A Catachresis … plus an Idea

"*Si au moins il y en avait moins*"—"*Je ne suis pas sûr que ça changerait quelque chose.*" In short, "less" is (not different from) "more"—hence the "*contradiction*" or, as Guattari labels it, the "*catachrèse.*"

It should be recalled here that, from 1961 to 1972, Guattari repeatedly tried to bring together the heterogeneous collection of desire's multiples (partial objects, nodal points, imaginary formations, etc.) under a single "Idea" (the term is Guattari's own, as is its capitalization). There are three key texts in this respect: *"D'un signe à l'autre"* (1961–6) which, originally published in vol. 2 of the journal *Recherches* (1966) and fragmentarily included in *Psychanalyse et transversalité* (henceforth *PT*, pp. 131–50), contains a series of jumbled reflections on Lacan's seminar on Poe's "purloined letter"[5] originally sent by Guattari to Lacan in a letter of December 8, 1961[6]; and two of the texts collected by Stéphane Nadaud in *Écrits pour L'anti-Œdipe* (henceforth *EAŒ*), namely, *"De deux types de coupures"* (= *EAŒ*, pp. 361–95) and *"Plan de consistence* (1972)" (= *EAŒ*, pp. 459–84).

In *"D'un signe à l'autre,"* Guattari asks himself whether it would be possible to form a "chain" out of a multiplicity of "signs" or "points" (lit., *"point-signes"*) each of which would exclusively refer to itself (*PT*, p. 133–4). Such "points" (to which no "task" can therefore be assigned within a whole [*PT*., pp. 131–2]) stand for desire's *minimal units* (*PT*, p. 135), which thus form a discrete multiplicity. It is not, then, that each "sign-point" is ideally united to others because, like them, it would be nothing else than an intensive modality of something that would, in turn, be nothing more than all such points (i.e., their mere collection) but would yet be too, if elusively, something else (something more), like Spinoza's substance according to Deleuze's interpretation of Spinoza.[7] Rather, says Guattari, each point can be *ideally* united to other points. Can it? he asks (*PT*, p. 134). It can, inasmuch as there is *nothing* else that links all such points, as each one refers but to itself (alone).[8] As in *Parménide*—whose scattered style it somehow resembles—the key issue in *"D'un signe à l'autre"* is then the relation between, or rather the coincidence of, the Many and the One: "[a]lternativement une et multiple [...]" (*PT*, p. 147).⁹

For its part, in "*Plan de consistence* (1972)" we read: "*Le plan de consistence* [cf. the notion of chain above] *est alors une Idée à la énième puissance qui intègre l'ensemble des puissances du disjoint*" (*EAŒ*, p. 483). We have here another of Guattari's early sketches of the co-implication of the One and the Many. It is therefore fair to ask how One and Many, Many and One, reflect one another, and whether their mutual reflection conceals their mutual refraction. For saying that the Multiple comes together exponentially under a single "Idea" is still saying too little. If all is One, how can it be Many? If it is Many, how can it be One? That is, what kind of "Idea" could effectively turn the Many into One and the One into Many? Furthermore, and to go back to the problem hinted at in the previous paragraph, should the One be thought in quantitative *or* qualitative terms? Should it be envisaged, that is, as a single being or substance with different quantitative expressive modalities, *or* should it be rather conceived as a single topological "plane" on which desire's constitutive elements would be distributed at different heights?

4 / On the Difference between Guattari's and Deleuze's Early Ontologies

A fine way to explore such questions would be to ask whether for Guattari *being* is said univocally, analogically, or equivocally of what is, i.e., whether it is said in identical, similar, or incommensurable terms of everything that is. Although we lack a straightforward answer thereof, there are good reasons to suspect that for Guattari *being is not said equally*, i.e., in the same way, of desire's multiples. Thus, for example, a passage in *L'anti-Œdipe* (henceforth *AŒ*) reads: "*les pièces ou éléments des machines désirantes se reconnaissent à leur indépendance mutuelle* [...] *Elles ne doivent pas être des déterminations opposes d'une même entité, ni les différenciations d'une être unique*, [...] *mais des différents ou des réellement-distincts, des « êtres » distincts*" (*AŒ*, p. 390). Conversely, in *Spinoza et le problème de l'expression* (p. 180), which predates *AŒ* by four years, Deleuze holds that all things are but the expressive modes of a single substance or being and that they differ from each other in intensive or quantitative rather than qualitative terms.[10] Accordingly, I take the aforementioned passage in *AŒ* to be a genuinely Guattarian passage that witnesses to a significant divergence between Guattari's and Deleuze's respective ontologies in the early stages of their collaboration. This contention is further supported, I think, by Guattari's distinction between "*signe-puissance*" and "*signe-figure*" in "*De deux types de coupures*," a text from 1971 that has not received due attention even though such divergence is quite patent in it.[11]

What does Guattari mean by these *two* different types of "signs"? Before responding to this question, allow me to stress that Guattari sees differences in exponential terms because, in principle, everything (i.e., desire's many options) is for him equally possible. This leads him to commend Spinoza's philosophy and Deleuze's interpretation of it in *EAŒ* (pp. 362, 367, 372–8), as for Spinoza and Deleuze being's expressive modalities are all on equal standing. Yet, unlike Deleuze, who—notwithstanding his brief comparative remarks on Spinoza and Leibniz in *Spinoza et le problème de l'expression*—would only go in depth into Leibniz in the late 1980s, in 1971 Guattari also vindicates Leibniz ... *contra* Spinoza. More exactly, he distinguishes between two different politics that, he says, ought to be combined: (*a*) Spinoza's "monist" politics (*EAŒ*, pp. 375–6), which aim, he says, at distributing "neutrally" all things by removing from reality any trace of transcendence,[12] i.e., by subsuming all things under a single substance[13]; and, as a counterpoint to it, (*b*) Leibniz's "monadic" politics, according to which substances are many instead, i.e., ontologically distinct from one another (like Leibniz's monads) and thus qualitatively unassimilable (*EAŒ*, pp. 367, 374, 376–9). For, in Leibniz, substances are, first and foremost, actions, and all actions are individual, for which reason there cannot be a common substance (Leibniz, *Monadology*, §§ 17–18)[14]; additionally, says Leibniz, all substances present singular traits, which makes it absurd to think of a single substance (§§ 9–13). "*Le pluralisme des substances est notre affaire*" whatever other philosophers might have made of it, writes Guattari (*EAŒ*, p. 367). It can hardly be put in more straightforward terms. For Guattari, then, what is common to all things is neither their being nor their substance: it is, rather, (α) their *there-ness*, since "plane" is above all a *topological* category, and (β) their equal *capacity* to increase (and decrease) their consistency, inasmuch as such plane is one of *consistency*—"plane of consistency" being therefore Guattari's originally "Idea" for "integrating the powers of the disjoint" (*EAŒ*, p. 483).

Leibniz therefore provides Guattari with what the latter calls a principle for the "brick-work" of "discrete figures" (*EAŒ*, p. 377), i.e., a principle for the ontological discrimination of desire's always-singular realities, which—this should be apparent by now—do *not* share the same being.[15] That is, whatever we fancy and/or do does not merely represent *a* wave among *other* waves in an ocean of possibilities: it is always *unique*. Guattari calls it a *figure*—or more to the point, and insofar as he views reality as a collection of distinct semiotic affordances,[16] a "figure-sign" (*signe-figure*) (*EAŒ*, p. 375; cf. the notion of "*point-signe*" in "*D'un signe à l'autre*"). Hence, on one level we have Spinoza's "power-signs" (*signes de puissance*) (*EAŒ*, pp. 321–59, 375), given that everything we fancy and/or do is equally possible and may empower us, albeit differently (unless it disempowers us, in which case we will have to opt for something else instead). But we also have, on another level, Leibniz's "figure-signs." These two types of signs, underlines Guattari, form a "*couple disjoint*" (*EAŒ*, 394) i.e., a "disjoint couple"—an expression that the English translation unduly simplifies as "pair."[17] In sum, we thought we were playing philosophy with only two cards: "One" and "Many," and all of a sudden, a third card—"Two"—asks us to make room for it.

5 / Back to the "*Truc*"

Back, that is, to our dialog: "*Un truc genre Parménide.*" A Parmenides-like "issue" or "thing"—but also "trick," as per the dual etymology of the French word *truc*—that, by rendering everything as one or gathering it all within a single plane (of consistency), does not really simplify anything, then. It rather signals a "threshold" ("*un seuil* […] *de la complexité*") which turns complexity and simplicity reciprocally inside out, so that what each one of them gains on one level is lost to its opposite on the other[18]:—"[S]"*il en avait moins …*

'—"*Alors, tu crois que ce serait plus simple !*"—"*Hé bé ... je vais te le dire,* [...] *pas du tout.*" As Lévi-Strauss would have it, One and Many stand here in "dynamic disequilibrium"—or, in other words, as the two sides of an endless chiasmus.

6 / Enters Junon

Again: the first twelve pages of Guattari's *Parménide* gravitate around this conceptual "truc"—assuredly a devilish or daimonic one, like the road taken by the charioteer in Parmenides' poem (frag. DK B1). And then *voilà*—without interruption: "[L]*e mystère de mes fesses.*"—"*C'est comme ça.*"—"*Il n'y a pas preneur ?*"

Put otherwise: "*Entré de Junon.*" A Goddess. Parmenides'? It looks like it, given that a *goddess* (Ἀλήθεια in Parmenides) awaits the charioteer at the *end* of the road that leads to her dwelling-place and to the philosophical core of the poem, and that here Junon leads the dialog's characters and the reader to the astounding (playful and provoking) end of the piece.[19] But not quite Parmenides', then! In any event, a major Olympic goddess (Juno or Hera) who thus *brings* the previous intellectual game to an end and that (like Parmenides' goddess, whose name is built after the verb λήθω [to "hide" or "conceal"] preceded by the privative prefix ἀ-) "discloses" something to us, inasmuch as she *substitutes*, as it were, one "*truc*" for another—a goddess, that is, *who turns the intellectual game* (*le* "*truc genre Parménide*") *inside out to extract from it its alleged reverse*: first it was the νοῦς—read (*contra* Lacan?): in the beginning it was the Logos—... now it is the flesh! And yet, *a reverse that paradoxically (magically?)*[20] *coincides with its obverse from all sides!* Plainly: BEING, OR DESIRE:: DESIRE, OR BEING—*both One and Many, Many and One.*

Apparently, then, not so much here Parmenides *as Parmenides' own reverse*, i.e., Heraclitus (DK B51): "οὐ ξυνιᾶσιν ὅκως διαφερόμενον ἑωυτῷ ὁμολογέει· παλίντροπος ἁρμονίη ὅκωσπερ τόξου καὶ λύρης" [they do not understand that what diverges coincides: bent-back attunement, like that of the bow and the lyre] (my trans.). But actually no, Heraclitus' obverse as well, i.e., Parmenides ... *Of course!* For what this new\old goddess discloses for us is *the view (read: the very truth) that* DESIRE *and* BEING *are* ONE: τὸ αὐτό, *"the same"* (Parmenides, DK B3)—*plus that they are the thinkable as such* (Parmenides, DK B3), i.e., what *stitches* the first half of the dialog (pp. 1–12 of the ms. reproduced in this book) onto the second one (pp. 12–14) and what, accordingly, keeps us reading *through* them.

But if DESIRE and BEING are ONE, what do we do with Lacan, and what do we do, then with Lacan's own take on desire as *lack*? One could, perhaps, write with it a subtitle for the piece, a subtitle for Guattari's *Parménide*—something, then, along these lines: "Farewell to Lacan."

Can you fancy anything more ... Guattarian?

7 / *Parménide* vis-à-vis *Socrate*

A *psychorama* (rather than a psychodrama!)[21] of "scattered words" and "jumbled thoughts": Flore Garcin-Marrou's brief, yet very-much-to-the-point, description of Guattari's *Socrate* is, I think, entirely applicable to Guattari's *Parménide*[22]—as also is Garcin-Marrou's overall remark that in Guattari's theatrical pieces theater is (pure) experimentation rather than (the) interpretation (of roles).[23] Both texts, therefore, share a common style. There is, however, a major difference between them—other than their very dissimilar length and the fact that in *Parménide* most characters lack name, that is. In *Socrate*, Socrates, the philosopher, is indirectly present through his (delirious) impersonation by one of the characters: "George." Conversely, in *Parménide*, Parmenides, the philosopher, is only present in the allusion to his name made by one of the (anonymous) characters and, additionally and most importantly, through the (at first sight nonsensical rather than properly delirious, though it all has its sense, as we have seen) re-problematization of *Parmenides' problem*: that of the Many and the One.

Actually, there is yet another salient difference between the two texts. In *Socrate*, Socrate is ridiculed.[24] In *Parménide*, Parmenides is apparently ridiculed: "*Si au moins il y en avait moins*"—"*Ah oui peut-être qu'on n'y retrouverait plus.*"—"*En quelque sorte …*"—"*Alors !*"—"*C'est pas évident.*"—"*Je ne suis pas sûr que ça changerait quelque chose.*"—"*Il n'y aurait plus qu'une chose et un seul truc pour regarder la chose.*"—"*Un truc genre Parménide.*"—"*Alors, tu crois que ce serait plus simple !*"—"*A priori … je ne sais pas.*"—"*Hé bé … je vais te le dire, hé bien, pas du tout, à mon avis, si tu veux savoir, je suis même sûr que pas de tout.*"— "*Tiens !*"—"*Bon !*"—"*Et si'l n'y avait qu'un seul truc. Mais, tu vois, vraiment qu'un seul !*"—"*Pauvre con !*" Yet, as I have argued, the dialog ends by tacitly identifying DESIRE and BEING—as One and as a One that is simultaneously Many. In other words, while Guattari's *Socrate* is not a Socratic text, Guattari's *Parménide* is—in its own peculiar but brilliant way—a Parmenidean text through and through.

Abbreviations

AŒ   *L'anti-Œdipe*
EAŒ   *Écrits pour L'anti-Œdipe*
PT   *Psychanalyse et transversalité*

Notes

1. Variants throughout the text: (*a*) "[S]"*il en avait moins peut-être que*'—"*Ah oui peut-être qu'on n'y retrouverait plus*"—"*C'est pas évident.*" (*b*) "*Alors, tu crois que ce serait plus simple !*"—"*Hé bé… je vais te le dire,* […] *pas du tout.*" Cf. Simondon's formula ("plus qu'unité, plus qu'identité") in *L'individu et sa genèse physico-biologique*, 24.

2. Cf. Deleuze, *Le Bergsonisme*, 6: "*il y a* non pas moins*, mais* plus *dans l'idée de non-être que dans celle d'être* […] *en effet, il y a l'idée d'être, plus une opération logique de négation généralisée.*"

3. Furthermore, Parmenides (in frag. DK B3) designates as νοῦς the "thought" of "being." Why? Because although it is through a dialectical process (as shown in §§*i–ii* above) that one is led to think about being's *oneness*, it is ultimately an "intuition" or "vision" (νοῦς) that discloses it for us (suddenly, we then "see"/realize that only "being" *is* and that "being" is *one*).

4. Crentone, "Introduzione" (to Plato's *Sophist*), xli.

5. Lacan, *Écrits*, 11–61.

6. See the (unnumbered) footnote in *PT*, 131.

7. Deleuze, *Spinoza et le problème de l'expression*, 153–96; *Spinoza. Philosophie pratique*, 118–20, 147–8.

8. "*Voici le signe. Le signe de rien. Un signe qui, ne renvoyant qu'à lui-même, ne renvoie à rien. Il porte le rien en son sein. Et, pour cette raison, il se lie sans difficulté aux autres signes, porteurs de la même néantité*" (*PT*, 133).

9. Cf. Guattari's own confession—which is, I think, very opportunely quoted by Stéphane Nadaud in his foreword to *EAŒ* (11–12) to outline the

different vital attitudes of Guattari and Deleuze against the backdrop of their encounter in 1969—regarding the different "places" where, at that time, Guattari deployed his political, medical, and theoretical activity (and hence too regarding his different "ways" of living); places which, he says, he felt he had to "glue together" without "unifying them." Theoretically speaking, the wish to find out the "coherence" of what "lacks" any *a-priori* "link" is already in Serge Leclaire, whom Guattari read attentively prior to the writing of *L'anti-Œdipe* (see *PT*, 139 n. 1; *EAŒ*, 168, 214, 238). Deleuze, too, mentions Leclaire in his early writings (see *Différence et Répétition*, 135 n. 1), but he does so only once and while commenting on the role that what is *absent* from it plays in the unconscious, which betrays Deleuze's initial Lacanian orientation (on which, see Collett, *The Psychoanalysis of Sense*). In this respect, the references to Leclaire in *AŒ* (on 369 n. 28, 370 n. 29, 375, 386–7) present hybrid traits combining Guattari and Deleuze's respective, but divergent, approaches to the Unity of the Many, on which, see the next section and n. 22 of the Foreword to the present volume.

10 Cf. too Deleuze's claim in *Différence et répétition* (53) that being must be said "univocally" of the different, "*comme le blanc se rapporte à des intensités diverses, mais reste essentiellement le même blanc.*"

11 See further Segovia, *Guattari beyond Deleuze*, 18–28, whose argument I am reproducing in this section in abridged form.

12 For Spinoza's God does not impose a selective plan upon what is, but amounts to the totality of what is, which is no longer judged, repressed, etc.

13 Hence, Spinoza's well-known formula: "*Deus sive Natura.*"

14 The term "monad" derives from the Greek μονάς: "unity"; it denotes something that stands "alone" insofar as it is "one" in the sense of unique: μόνος.

15 As of today, however, Guattari's indebtedness to Leibniz remains underrated. Thus, Leibniz's name is absent from Gary Genosko's otherwise excellent 2012 introduction to Guattari's thought. In Eugene B. Young, Gary Genosko, and Janell Watson's one-volume Deleuzian-Guattarian dictionary (2013), Leibniz is solely introduced in relation to Deleuze's philosophy (Young, "Leibniz, Gottfried Wilhelm"). In Éric Alliez and Andrew Goffey's 2011 edited volume, *The Guattari Effect*, it is mentioned by Raymond Bellour in his essay on Guattari and cinema, but in connection with Deleuze and Whitehead (Bellour, "Going to the Cinema with Félix Guattari and Daniel Stern," 233). Only Janell Watson did, in 2009, allude to Leibniz as one of Guattari's early sources

(Watson, *Guattari's Diagrammatic Thought*, 155). More recently, Hanjo Berressem, in his 2020 study on Guattari's ecosophy, pays tribute to Leibniz's influence on Guattari, but he deals mostly with Guattari's later works, such as *Cartographies schizoanalytiques* (Berressem, *Guattari's Schozoanalytic Ecology*, 155–80). Lastly, Manola Antonioli—one of the contributors to Thomas Jellis, Joe Gerlach, and J. D. Dewsbury's recently edited volume, *Why Guattari?* (2019)—rightly claims that Guattari's concept of the unconscious differs from Leibniz's concept of monad in that the unconscious, for Guattari, is not closed upon itself (Antonioli, "Mapping the Unconscious," 36). Closure is indeed what Guattari rejects from Leibniz's monadology. Yet, one should not lose sight of the fact that, as Deleuze has it, "*la force d'une philosophie se mesure aux concepts qu'elle crée, ou dont elle renouvelle le sens*" (Deleuze, *Spinoza et le problème de l'expression*, 299). Guattari thus reuses Leibniz in his own creative way.

16 On which, see, e.g., Guattari, *L'inconscient machinique*, 223–54.

17 Guattari, *The Anti-Oedipus Papers*, 278.

18 To paraphrase Lévi-Strauss in "Reciprocity and Hierarchy," 268.

19 Besides, this is not the only occasion in which Guattari plays with ancient-Greek goddesses; see Guattari's own reference to Ananke, Dike, Moira, and Hybris (as notional permutations of his F, Φ, U, and T ontological functors) in *Cartographies schizoanalytiques*, 217, 234.

20 Cf. Deleuze & Guattari, *Mille plateaux*, 31: "[l]*a formule magique que nous cherchons tous.*"

21 The term "psychorama" is used by "Carmen" in her final intervention in Guattari's *Socrate*.

22 Garcin-Marrou, "To Be or not to Be Socrates," 23.

23 Ibid.

24 Garcin-Marrou (ibid., 23–4) draws well the parallel with his portrayal in Aristophanes. But Nietzsche could also be evoked here!

References

Alliez, Éric, and Andrew Goffey (eds.), *The Guattari Effect*, London: Continuum, 2011.

Antonioli, Manola, "Mapping the Unconscious," in *Why Guattari? A Liberation of Cartographies, Ecologies and Politics*, ed. Thomas Jellis, Joe Gerlach, and J. D. Dewsbury, London: Routledge, 2019, 34–44.

Bellour, Raymond, "Going to the Cinema with Félix Guattari and Daniel Stern," in *The Guattari Effect*, ed. Éric Alliez and Andrew Goffey, London: Continuum, 2011, 220–34.

Berressem, Hanjo, *Guattari's Schozoanalytic Ecology*, Edinburgh: Edinburgh University Press, 2020.

Centrone, Bruno, "Introduzione," in Platone, *Sofista*, ed. Bruno Centrone, Turin: Einaudi, 2008, i–lxxv.

Collett, Guillaume, *The Psychoanalysis of Sense: Deleuze and the Lacanian School*, Edinburgh: Edinburgh University Press, 2016.

Deleuze, Gilles, *Le Bergsonisme*, Paris: Presses Universitaires de France, 1966.

Deleuze, Gilles, *Spinoza et le problème de l'expression*, Paris: Presses Universitaires de France, 1968.

Deleuze, Gilles, *Spinoza. Philosophie pratique*, Paris: Les Éditions de Minuit, 1972.

Deleuze, Gilles, and Félix Guattari, *L'Anti-Œdipe: Capitalisme et schizophrénie 1*, Paris: Les Éditions de Minuit, 1972.

Deleuze, Gilles, and Félix Guattari, *Mille plateaux: Capitalisme et schizophrénie 2*, Paris: Les Éditions de Minuit, 1980.

Garcin-Marrou, Flore, "To Be or not to Be Socrates: Introduction to the Translation of Félix Guattari's Socrates," *Deleuze and Guattari Studies*, vol. 2 6/2 (2012): 22–4.

Genosko, Gary, *Félix Guattari: An Aberrant Introduction*, London: Continuum, 2002.

Guattari, Félix, *L'inconscient machinique: Essais de schizo-analyse*, Paris: Éditions Recherches, 1979.

Guattari, Félix, *Psychanalyse et transversalité: Essais d'analyse institutionnelle*, Préface de Gilles Deleuze, nouvelle édition, Paris: La Découverte, 2003.

Guattari, Félix, *Écrits pour L'Anti-Œdipe*, ed. Stéphane Nadaud, Paris: Éditions Lignes/Manifeste, 2004.

Guattari, Félix, *The Anti-Oedipus Papers*, ed. Stéphane Nadaud, trans. Kelina Gotman, Los Angeles, CA: Semiotext(e), 2006.

Kirk, G. S., J. E. Raven, and M. Schofield, *The Pre-Socratic Philosophers: A Critical History with a Selection of Texts*, second edition, Cambridge: Cambridge University Press, 1983.

Lacan, Jaques, *Écrits*, Paris: Seuil, 1966.

Leclaire, Serge, *Écrits pour la psychanalyse*, 2 vols., Paris: Seuil, 1996–8.

Leibniz, Gottfried Wilhelm, *Monadology: A New Translation and Guide*, trans. Lloyd Strickland, Edinburgh: Edinburgh University Press, 2014.

Lévi-Strauss, Claude, "Reciprocity and Hierarchy," *American Anthropologist* 46 (1944): 266–8.
Nadaud, Stéphane. "Les amours d'une guêpe et d'une orchidée," in Félix Guattari, *Écrits pour L'Anti-Œdipe*, ed. Stéphane Nadaud, Paris: Éditions Lignes & Manifeste, 2004, 7–31.
Segovia, Carlos A., *Guattari beyond Deleuze: Ontology and Modal Philosophy in Guattari's Major Writings*, London: Palgrave Macmillan, 2024.
Simondon, Gilbert. *L'individu et sa genèse physico-biologique*, préface de Jacques Garelli, Grenoble: Millon, 1995.
Spinoza, Baruch, *Ethics, Proved in Geometrical Order*, ed. Matthew J. Kisner, trans. Michael Silverthorne and Matthew J. Kisner, Cambridge: Cambridge University Press, 2018.
Watson, Janell, *Guattari's Diagrammatic Thought: Writing between Lacan and Deleuze*, London: Continuum, 2009.
Young, Eugene B., "Leibniz, Gottfried Wilhelm," in *The Deleuze and Guattari Dictionary*, ed. Eugene B. Young with Gary Genosko and Janell Watson, London: Bloomsbury, 2013, 177–9.

10

Guattari's Constructivism and the Theater Machine of Revolution

Mahoro Murasawa

Foreword

The plays *Parmenides* and *Socrates* by Guattari in this book not only show that in his later years Guattari had a strong interest in ancient Greek thought, but also suggest that "theater" was an extremely privileged artistic field for him and that it was key to the expression of his thought. In examining his two plays, this chapter will first refer to Guattari's four-quadrant diagram and briefly summarize two important perspectives for understanding Guattari's thought: philosophical and political, respectively. Next, the ideological importance of theater for Guattari will be clarified, with reference to the idea of "constructivism," an artistic current in the Russian Revolution. Finally, I will briefly discuss the two plays in the light of these arguments.

1 / Theater as Machine of Revolution

In an interview with butoh dancer Min Tanaka in June 1984, Guattari asked Tanaka the following questions[1]:

(1) Is Min Tanaka's dance (butoh) on a "molecular level" or is it "highly developed and purposeful"?

(2) How does the dimension of horizontality (the "becoming animal" of Min Tanaka) relate to the dimension of verticality (the "changing arrangement of the constellations of universes")?

As a reason for asking those questions, Guattari cites his concern with the following issues:

(a) What is the relationship between theatrical space and physical intensity?

(b) What are the linking elements between the discursive realm (or the world of representation) and the realm of the "body without organs" (or the production of the real) ?

Guattari further explains why he was interested in Min Tanaka's dance as follows:

> There is an extreme delicacy in [Min Tanaka's] butoh. His dance is at the opposite end of the expressive and painful relationship with the body that is in the mythic action specific to the student movement of 1968.[2]

This interview took place five years before the publication of Guattari's *Schizoanalytic Cartographies*, but it is easy to see that Guattari had developed the prototype of the four-quadrant diagram at this point (Figure 1). With reference to his diagram, Guattari's two questions to Min Tanaka can be paraphrased as follows:

(1') Does Min Tanaka's butoh remain at the micro (T and F) level, or does it reach the macro (Φ and U) level?

(2') How does the new T (existential territory) generated by the "becoming animal" in Min Tanaka's butoh cause changes in U (the immaterial universe)?

These two questions boil down to the twin question of how molecular changes in the micro (F and T) cause changes in the macro (Φ and U). As mentioned above, given that Guattari here contrasted Min Tanaka's dance with the revolutionary student movement of 1968, and given that Guattari advocated the revolution of subjectivity (molecular revolution) through his reflections on the failure of the revolution of 1968, the question he was considering in this interview is clear: What are the conditions for developing a revolution of individual subjectivity (molecular revolution) into a revolution of society as a whole (political revolution)?

Guattari's schema in *Schizoanalytic Cartographies* (1989)

	actual	virtual	
possible	Φ (phylum)	U (immaterial universe)	macro
real	F (flow)	T (existential territory)	micro
	objective/discursive	subjective/existential	

Figure 1 Guattari's schizoanalysis, as synthesized by the author (esp. after figs. 1 & 2 [French ed.] = figs. 1.1 & 1.2 [English ed.] of Guattari's *Schizoanalytic Cartographies*).

It is interesting to note here that in (a) above Guattari contrasted the theatrical space with the realm of physical intensity. This is because it can be seen that, for Guattari, the micro-subjective (and existential) revolution at the level of physical intensity corresponds to Min Tanaka's dance (butoh), while the revolution of society as a whole is seen as corresponding to "theater."

Another of Guattari's concerns (b) is closely related to this issue. This is because theater "creates a new existential territory through the transformation of the semiotic elements of the discursive realm."[3]

What this shows is that, first, for Guattari, theater was not only a branch of art, but also a prototype of the "machine" that transforms a subjective (spiritual) revolution into an objective (social) revolution. Secondly, Guattari's four-quadrant diagram was not only a therapeutic theory in psychiatry but was conceived from the outset as a theory of social revolution. Therefore, Guattari's theater-related practice in his later years should be interpreted as an extension of the theoretical consideration of the four-quadrant diagram, and at the same time as a theoretical exploration of social revolution.

2 / Guattari as Constructivist

A social revolution cannot be achieved simply by a revolution in the existential and subjective sphere (creation of existential territories and new arrangement of constellations in the immaterial universe). This is because that would be no different from an individual moral reform. On the contrary, a revolution in the discursive and objective realm (political revolution or social revolution) will not lead to any solution unless there is a revolution in the discursive and subjective realm. In this type of revolution, the form of society may change, but the content of society remains the same.

What distinguishes Guattari from Spinoza and Bergson (and to some extent Deleuze) ideologically is that he does not reduce the former to the latter, or emphasize only the latter and neglect the former, with regard to the two domains of the discursive-objective and existential-subjective. For many philosophers, the latter is more important, and the former, as a matter of social and cultural institutions, is usually not of interest because it is the domain of semioticians, economists, and sociologists. However, as a practitioner, Guattari was deeply aware of the importance of the former and continued to pursue its theoretical possibilities. This is inseparable from his interest in "institutions," as he was deeply involved in institutionalist psychotherapy.

This interest in institutions overlaps considerably with the ideas of the Russian Constructivist artists: in the Russian Revolution of the early twentieth century, the Constructivists tried to create, through art, the basic ideas of a new social system that would break away from the capitalist system. This was one end point of Western modern art beginning in the nineteenth century.

Modern Western European painting after the French Revolution was a history of battles with the Academy of Fine Arts and a pathway away from its aesthetic norms. The Academy's aesthetic norm, neoclassicism, was extremely Kantian. In painting, the emphasis was on the precise drawing of the subject and the line (contour) was most important. Vivid colors were rejected and color was regarded as subordinate to line. The image created by precise lines and subdued colors was considered to be a painting. The Academy's perspective of line/image/color overlaps directly with the distinction between reason/understanding/sensibility in Kant's philosophy. This is because "line" in painting corresponds to "form" in philosophy, while "color" corresponds to "matter."

In the first half of the nineteenth century, Delacroix and other Romantic artists were the first opponents of such Kantian norms of the Academy. They saw that the aesthetic norms of the Academy were directly linked to the ideology of statism. There, the essence of society was regarded as the "state (institution)" and the people ought to subordinate to it. In other words, the distinction between reason/understanding/sensibility in Kant's philosophy was epistemologically identical to the distinction between line/image/color in painting and the distinction between state/assembly/people as institutions in society. Delacroix's assertion that color is the essence of painting directly reflected his revolutionary ideas that the people are the essence of society and that the state should be subordinate to the people.

After Romanticism, in Western European avant-garde art, the emancipation of painting from the rigid norms of the academy proceeded in deep connection with the emancipation of the people from the rigid institutions of the bourgeois capitalist state. It culminated in German Expressionism. Kandinsky proclaimed the "emancipation of color from the line" in painting, rearranging the colors that had been confined within the contours of the subject, in musical harmony. This was an attempt to explore, in the sensory dimension, the possibility of liberating the people, who were suffering from the institutional exploitation of the capitalist state, in a new harmonious society.

However, for the artists of the revolutionary period in Russia, Kandinsky was inadequate in two respects. First, the Russian Revolution aimed not only to liberate the people from the existing institutions of the capitalist state, but also to include them in the new institutions of the new communist state. In painting, this meant that it was necessary not only to liberate color from the line, but also to encompass it within a new line. Thus, Russian avant-garde artists worked to redefine the "line." Rodchenko abandoned the perspective of the line as a "contour" that confines color, and redefined the line as an element that constitutes a plane or a three-dimensional object. This new perspective (Rodchenko called it "line-ism" or "lineaism") led them to call themselves Constructivists and liberate paintings from two-dimensional canvas into three-dimensional architecture and material products.

Secondly, in Kandinsky's view, art remained a means of subjectively expressing the artist's inner life. However, Russian artists considered art to be an objective means of expressing society outside the artist. In other words, art had to be transformed into something that could be expressed according to objective conditions such as science and technology, budget, supply, and demand. Thus, the Constructivists repositioned product design and industrial production as new art:

> Constructivism can and must take into account all the concrete demands of modern life. It must also answer perfectly to the demands of the mass consumer, the collective, the customer, i.e. the people.[4]

In short, in Russian Constructivist thought, expressionism, which liberated color from the line, was a necessary but not sufficient condition for their new art. Breaking away from the capitalist state was a necessary but not sufficient condition for their revolution. And breaking away from Kantian philosophy was a necessary but not sufficient condition for their new thought. It lacked a new line, that is, a new system, a new form (idea). From this perspective, Bergson was clearly expressionist (in fact the German expressionists were greatly influenced by his thought), and relatively so was Deleuze.[5] However, Guattari clearly stands on the side of Russian Constructivism in that he aimed not only to liberate himself from existing institutions, but also to construct new institutions from them. For Guattari, the transformation of subjectivity (molecular revolution) was a necessary but not sufficient condition for social revolution. And it was that sufficient condition that the late Guattari explored.

3 / On Guattari's *Parmenides*: Exorcising the One

In light of the relationship between Guattari's four-quadrant diagram and social revolution, as well as Guattari's constructivist philosophical features described above, let us consider the subject matter of two of Guattari's plays, in particular *Parmenides*.[6]

Parmenides is known as an ancient Greek philosopher who stated that "what exists exists and what does not exist does not exist," denied generative change or "becoming" as a process whereby "what did not exist comes to exist" and insisted that the unchanging and immortal "One" is the true reality. In Guattari's plays, the characters debate over how to recognize the One. As such, they take the viewpoint that generative change is a false reality, or in other words, a "multiple" subordinate to the "One."

Here, Parmenides' thought can be interpreted from the standpoint of idealism, from Plato to Kant. From that perspective, many cups in the world are false realities, and the only true reality of the cup is the "Cup" as an idea. This corresponds to the neoclassical perspective of the Academy in painting (the contour line is the essence of painting and color should serve the line) and the nationalist perspective in politics (the state as an institution is the essence of society and the people should serve the state).

On the other hand, Parmenides' thought can also be interpreted as a Spinozist monism of the Substance (as God-Nature). From this perspective, all the things that make up the complexity of the world are merely the myriad diverse appearances of a single Substance reflecting itself in an infinite mirror. For him, the recognition of that single entity is a necessary and sufficient condition for man to live a true life. Then, both recognizing the complex things of this world and living among them become meaningless to him. This is much like the attitude of the Zen Buddhist monk. He alone escapes from the prison of this human world and goes outside it (Nature), never to return. And he leaves the prison remain a prison.

Whether the One was an idea or a substance for Parmenides, we cannot know. In any case, everything takes a turn when Juno appears at the end of Guattari's play: she tempts the characters to stop arguing and have intercourse with her, stirring up their desires. Thus, they forget that they were looking for the "One." In other words, just as they were trying to escape the prison of complexity of the multiple in search of the One, they are confronted with a fundamental question. Was it really a prison? Was it a false world, as Parmenides would say? Is it neither a prison nor a false world, but the true world, the very place where we live in reality?

Here, the characters are at the crossroads of whether a revolution of subjectivity will take place. Do they escape from this world full of falsehood and illusion and aim for the only reality, the One, or is the One illusion and this world real? If they choose the former, no change occurs to them. They will close their ears to Juno's siren song and, like the Argonauts, will single-mindedly aim for the One and leave this world. If they choose the latter, they will surrender to Juno's invitation and remain in this world. And they will exorcise the curse of the One. Whether this will be toward a social revolution that dismantles existing institutions, or toward an ideological revolution that dismantles the only entity, we do not know. In any case, there can be no doubt that Guattari thought there would be a revolution ahead.

Acknowledgment

I would like to thank Research Institute for International Society and Cultures at Ryukoku University for supporting the research project that formed the basis for this manuscript.

Notes

1. This text was published in the following book in Japanese, with no record of the original French version: Félix Guattari and Min Tanaka, *Light Speed and Zen Flame*(光速と禅炎), Tokyo: Asahi Shuppan, 1985. An English translation can be found in Félix Guattari, Machinic Eros: Writings on Japan, ed. Gary Genosko and Jay Hetrick, Minneapolis: Univocal, 2015, 45–53. For this paper I have used the original Japanese text.

2. Ibid., 8 (words in brackets supplemented by the author).

3. Ibid., 12.

4. Yakov Chernikhov, *The Construction of Architectural and Machine Forms*, Leningrad: Leningrad Association of Architects, 1931.

5. Such a contrast is examined from a philosophical perspective by Carlos A. Segovia in *Guattari beyond Deleuze: Ontology and Modal Philosophy in Guattari's Major Writings*, London: Palgrave Macmillan, 2025.

6. I have chosen to focus on Guattari's *Parmenides* here because it is simpler in structure than his *Socrates*, which is full of humor and irony, and its subject matter is simple and straightforward. Nevertheless, it should be clear to the reader that what I discussed here about the *Parmenides* is directly applicable to *Socrates*. Guattari's biting irony toward Lacan, Saussure and Klein in *Socrates* reflects the critical ideas of Guattari's psychoanalysis, and Lacan and his friends are identified with those who are obsessed with the One in *Parmenides*.

References

Chernikhov, Yakov, *The Construction of Architectural and Machine Forms*, Leningrad: Leningrad Association of Architects, 1931.

Guattari, Félix, and Min Tanaka, *Light Speed and Zen Flame* (光速と禅炎), Tokyo: Asahi Shuppan, 1985.

Segovia, Carlos A., *Guattari beyond Deleuze: Ontology and Modal Philosophy in Guattari's Major Writings*, London: Palgrave Macmillan, 2024.

11

The Trouble with People and Things

Iloe Ariss

Félix Guattari's short dialogic skit entitled *Parménide* or *Parmenides* after the pre-Socratic philosopher begins by identifying the problem: people and things, and all the rest. The dialog follows a roughly similar trajectory to Plato's dialog of the same name. First, the question of plurality arises, followed by the possibility of the one and the conditions of its existence. Then, when further speculation renders the one impossible, the interlocutors are forced to begin from the premise that the one *is*. Guattari's dialog supposes that if there is to be only one something, it would be a thing. He sometimes uses the French word *chose* to describe a "thing" but more often the word which appears in the dialog is *truc*. The word *chose* designates a specific item, and has a real object as referent, whereas *truc* applies to a general idea of thingness. If one forgets the name of a thing it automatically becomes *truc*, which can also be used to describe an action or process. In the German translation, I have attempted to retain this difference in terms through the use of *Sache* for *chose* and *Ding* for *truc*. *Ding* already has a lineage in German philosophy, from figures such as Kant and Heidegger. The thingness of things has been thoroughly elaborated in Heidegger's essay "Das Ding" as well as the etymology of the word thing, and its relationship to the world. For Heidegger, humanity itself is implied in the thing. It seems to contain every-thing within it. And things appear to be existent and perceptible, for Heidegger, whereas Guattari's dialog argues: if there were just one thing, we could not see it or know it.

Throughout the dialog, the interlocutors question whether "things" would be better if there were fewer of them. The first line reads, in my German translation "So eine Ansammlung,"[1] which translates "Toute cette accumulation." The German *Ansammlung*, meaning a gathering, aggregation, accumulation, shares its root with the word *Versammlung*, meaning assembly, gathering, assemblage. Both *Ansammlung* and *Versammlung* involve a bringing together of disparate entities into a collective. But the two seem to have an opposite meaning in that the parts of *Ansammlung* remain separate while in a group, whereas the entities gathered in a *Versammlung* fuse into a unified whole. Heidegger uses the latter word to define the thing in his essay, "Unsere Sprache nennt, was Versammlung ist in einem alten Wort. Dieses lautet: thing."[2] For Heidegger, a *Versammlung* is a unified object consisting of many parts which come together in a single thing, and in Guattari's dialogs, the opposite, a collection of disparate things, is called an *Ansammlung*. Guattari seems to maintain the opposition between the two terms, at least at the beginning. However, the phonetic interchangeability of these two terms suggests that there is no possibility of one without the many, or that, one thing does in fact mean many. They belong together paradoxically. Guattari's interlocutors notice this: there appear to be many things, but what if there were actually only one thing? This question mimics Plato's original dialog *Parmenides*, in which the character Parmenides states:

Take, if you like, the supposition that Zeno made—"*If there is a plurality of things.*"

You must consider what consequences must follow both for those many things with reference to one another and to the one, and also for the one with reference to itself and to the many. Then again, on the supposition that *there is not a plurality*, you must consider what will follow both for the one and for the many, with reference to themselves and each other.[3]

Guattari's dialog begins with a similar premise and traces the consequences. First, one interlocutor wonders whether things would be simpler if there were fewer of them, beginning with the assumption that there are indeed, many. They are unsure if this would be the case, so they explore the possibilities. However, there are already conditions placed on the idea of there only being one thing: "Schau mal. Es wäre nicht mehr als eine Sache und ein einzelnes Ding, damit die Sache anzugucken."[4] This first proposition retains the use of *chose* or *Sache*. If there were to be the one thing, it would have to be seen and looked at to confirm its existence—but then there would be another thing which does the looking, meaning there are already two things. In the following sentence, the dialog has already moved on to assuming the one thing which would exist is the thing that does the looking: "Ein Ding des Genres Parmenides."[5] The switch from *Sache* to *Ding* demonstrates the movement from perceptible object to conceptual thing. The next line responds to the suggestion of a Parmenidean thing, with "Nicht unbedingt."[6] In German, the play on words of the double negative implies that in fact, it is "bedingt" (it is necessary, or conditioned) that there be one and only one thing, and that that thing be a *Ding*.

They then begin to take this proposition seriously, "Und, wenn es nur ein Ding gäbe. Aber, schau mal, wirklich nur das eine!"[7] This elicits derision from another interlocutor: "armer Kerl."[8] While in Plato's dialog the fact that the one *is* causes it to topple into the many. The argument begins with the assertion that "if there is a *one*, of course the one will not be many. Consequently, it cannot have any parts or be a whole."[9] But, if the one is indeed in existence, "if a one *is*" then it fails to be a one because it must be composed of parts:

> Let us, then, once more state what will follow, if a one is. Consider whether this supposition does not necessarily imply that the one is such as to have parts. That follows in this way. Since "is" is asserted to belong to this *one* which is, and "one" is asserted to belong to this *being* which is one, and since "being" and "one" are not the same thing, but both belong to the same thing, namely that "one which is," that we are supposing, it follows that it is "one being" as a whole, and "one" and "being" will be its parts. So we must speak of each of these parts, not merely as a part, but as part of a whole.[10]

The existence of the one seems to necessitate the existence of the many. If the one has any characteristic whatsoever aside from oneness, then it must be more than one. Hence, the characteristic of being does not allow it to remain one. The very condition that the one *is* requires it to be more than one. Guattari also arrives at this point in a more absurd fashion:

> ... du hast gerade gesagt, dass es vielleicht komplizierter werden könnte ... Erinnerst du
> dich daran ...
> — Das ist nicht die Frage.
> — Doch, du hast von Parmenides' Schwelle der Komplexität gesprochen.[11]

They surmise it might become more complicated, if there is only one thing. Apparently, the threshold of complexity arrives early with the first characteristic of the one: being. One thing existing should not be as complicated as many things existing, and yet even with just the one, things do not become simpler, but rather problems proliferate. And thus, the existence of the one becomes the basis for the existence of the many. This is the trajectory of the Platonic dialog as well which concludes:

> So if there is no one, none of the others can be so much as imagined to be one, nor yet to be many, for you cannot imagine many without a one ... nor yet, if there is no one, can the others be or appear like or unlike or the same or different, or in contact or apart.[12]

In order for there to be many, there first needs to be a one, without the one, nothing can exist or be differentiated from each other. Things will not appear similar or different, unified or divided. Guattari evokes this conclusion in the inability to differentiate between the speakers in the dialog; the reader cannot know if it is one person talking to himself, two people, or in fact several. This quote also brings the person back into the understanding of the one. If there is one, someone needs to imagine it or it needs to appear to someone. But a refusal to do this, to imagine or perceive the one would be tantamount to its nonexistence, as another interlocutor clarifies: "Wenn ich gesagt habe, dass ich nicht mehr etwas bin in Bezug auf dein Ding."[13] If a person is no longer in relation to the thing, there can be no thing. The person either must be part of it, meaning there are parts and it is not one, or be completely consumed by it, meaning there is no person to see it. The distance of vision is necessary for establishing the existence of the thing. Guattari corroborates this: "Egal, das Ding ist, wenn es nur ein Ding gäbe, wäre niemand dabei, um das zu wissen usw …."[14] If no one is there to see the thing and know that it is one, then it is not a thing.

In Heidegger's essay "Das Ding," he includes Kant's view on this subject which happens to argue the exact opposite:

> Das Ding an sich bedeutet für Kant: der Gegenstand an sich. Der Charakter des »An- sich« besagt für Kant, daß der Gegenstand an sich Gegenstand ist ohne die Beziehung auf das menschliche Vorstellen, d. h. ohne das »Gegen«, wodurch er für dieses Vorstellen allererst steht. »Ding an sich« bedeutet, streng kantisch gedacht, einen Gegenstand, der für uns keiner ist, weil er stehen soll ohne ein mögliches Gegen: für das menschliche Vorstellen, das ihm entgegnet.[15]

According to Heidegger's summary of Kant, a thing is much more a thing-in-itself when it is not perceived or encountered by a human. But as a "Gegenstand," there needs to be something with which it is "gegen" (against). The statement of the interlocutor "Wenn ich gesagt habe, dass ich nicht mehr etwas bin in Bezug auf dein Ding,"[16] as I interpreted it above, seemed to deny the existence of the thing if it were not in relation to a person. However, this sentence can also be read in agreement with Kant's view, that in order for a thing to be a thing in itself, the person should not be involved with it. Accor(ding)ly, the human is no longer in relation to the thing, such that it can be a thing by and in-itself. But the use of the possessive pronoun *dein* (your) is unusual as it does not occur in relation to *Ding* in any other part of the dialog. Right before this line, it seems to be the same interlocutor who states, "es scheint mir, offen gesagt, dass du das in den falschen Hals gekriegt hast, weil du mich nicht ganz verstanden hast."[17] That is, he has not been understood and therefore wants nothing to do with *your* thing. The malleability of *truc* and *Ding* also becomes more apparent here, because they can stand in, even more broadly for a "way" of doing things, a "method" or "concept." The thing becomes personal, as the interlocutor does not agree with his (interlocutor's) *way of doing things,* but is only interested in (the) one thing.

Heidegger argues that a thing's nearness and presence are established by the thing (itself), implying the existence of both human and thing. Earlier, it was suggested in Guattari's dialog that the thing is also looking. The thing requires distance with which to see, too. But it cannot be too far away (whereas Kant's thing hides from perception in order to continue being itself). For Heidegger, "Das Ding ist nicht »in« der Nähe, als sei diese ein Behälter. Nähe waltet im Nähern als das Dingen des Dinges. Dingend verweilt das Ding die einigen Vier, Erde und Himmel, die Göttlichen und die Sterblichen, in der Einfalt ihres aus sich her einigen Gevierts."[18] The thing is not nearby as if nearness were a container or specific area in which the thing had to be found, but nearness prevails in drawing near (or nearing), just as the thinging of the thing gives it thingness. Somewhat suddenly, Heidegger includes in the identity of *Ding*, four things which are much larger than it: earth, heaven, the divine, and mortals. The expansive quality of the thing seems to overextend its limits in its relation to all these other things. These four elements of the thing fold into it, and are not to be understood as parts, but rather as acting within and through the thing. Heidegger explains:

> Das Ding verweilt das Geviert. Das Ding dingt Welt. Jedes Ding verweilt das Geviert in ein je Weiliges aus Einfalt der Welt. Wenn wir das Ding in seinem Dingen aus derweltenden Welt Wesen lassen, denken wir an das Ding als das Ding. Dergestalt andenkend lassen wir uns vom weltenden Wesen des Dinges angehen. So denkend sind wir vom Ding als dem Ding gerufen. Wir sind—im strengen Sinne des Wortes—die Be-Dingten.[19]

He argues that these four important elements of the world and humanity—heaven, earth, the divine, and mortals—linger in the thing, they are part of it in some way, but not in such a way that it should be composed of parts or a whole, as is the problem in Plato's *Parmenides*. Only when we let the thing be itself in the world in which it is a thing, can we also conceive of it as a thing. In that case, we are approached by the thing as a world-ing being. We are thinkingly called by the thing as a thing. Humans are surrounded, called, and made of the world by things, conditioned by things.

In this way, one of the interlocutors is in agreement with Heidegger when he says in the case of there being only one thing, "Na gut, doch nicht, meine Meinung nach, wenn du wissen möchtest, ich bin mir sicher, dass es keineswegs einfacher wäre."[20] It turns out that having only one thing does not make things less complicated in any way—rather, more interconnected. The complexity of *Ding* in Heidegger is reflected in the ever-increasing conditions of the one in Plato's *Parmenides*:

> The one has no shape, it is not either round or straight ... it cannot be anywhere, for it cannot be either (a) in another, or (b) in itself ... the one is immovable in respect to every kind of motion ... Nor can it be other than another, so long as it is one ... nor yet can it be the same as itself ... nor can the one be (a) like or (b) unlike anything ... therefore the one in no sense *is*.[21]

This is the first attempt in the dialog to define the one through privation, that is, through what it is not and cannot be, which arrives at the conclusion that it *is* not. However, neither Parmenides nor Aristotle (his partner in the dialog) is satisfied with this conclusion: "Now can this possibly be the case with the one? I do not think so, said Aristotle."[22] Then, the two decide to proceed from a new hypothesis that the one *is*. Similarly, Guattari's dialog continually returns to its premise (if there is only one thing) until a sudden break where the first named character arrives.

The Roman goddess Juno enters the scene, and appears to offer herself up sexually to the interlocutors, although nothing takes place. She then provides a demonstration which involves:

Wenn ich meine Hand zwischen die
Hoden_____Wenn ich mich
durchdrehe_____ein bisschen
überall_____nein wirklich_____?[23]

And one interlocutor interjects, "Wir sehen nicht, was du demonstrieren willst_____!"[24] Not only is this comical, but it also suggests that Juno is showing the men the one thing that they cannot see or imagine. If this is the one thing that exists, then they are unable to see, recognize, or know it. On the other hand, it is very difficult to make sense of this seemingly completely unrelated ending. Both associatively and anachronistically this ending reminds me of a meme that circulated in 2017 and the following years, primarily on Twitter (now X). The caption, from the original tweet, reads "guys literally only want one thing and it's fucking disgusting," but the meme-ification involves pairing this phrase with a harmless or absurdist image, such as a type of food, a nonsexual movie, a political goal, or gaining points in a video game, essentially anything that is not the implied thing in the tweet, that is, sex. Perhaps Guattari prematurely made this kind of joke at the end of the dialog. If there really only is one thing, these interlocutors would want it to be sex, with a goddess no less. But the joke is on them, because whatever she demonstrates, they cannot see what it is and therefore are not privy to the one thing. Or again, the premise of there only being one thing is forgotten the moment another thing appears.

Another possible explanation for this ending is an inter-text with Heidegger. In his *Vorlesungen* on Parmenides, Heidegger repeatedly makes the point that "truth" in Parmenides' original Ancient Greek poem *is* a goddess. Though his argument on this point changes throughout his lecture, the first iteration reads:

Die Göttin ist die Göttin "Wahrheit." Sie selbst—"die Wahrheit"—ist die Göttin. Wir vermeiden daher die Wendung, die von einer Göttin "der" Wahrheit sprechen möchte.[25]

If this logic is applied to the goddess in Guattari's dialog, Juno would not just represent an abstract concept but *be* that concept. Is she also truth, just as in Parmenides' original poem? Or is Guattari making a play on words from Heidegger's literal translation of *aletheia* into "Unverborgenheit," because Juno in the dialog is certainly unconcealed, in fact she exposes herself, saying "Das Rätsel meines Pos!"[26] Could Guattari crudely be referring to her "unconcealedness"?

While both mysteries remain, Heidegger's texts on Parmenides and "Das Ding" help to animate Guattari's dialog and Plato's *Parmenides* offers insight into similar considerations of the characteristics and consequences of there only being one thing. The end of the dialog does not arrive at an answer but perhaps at a kind of unconcealing, and the final cry from off-stage "Antworten Sie nicht darauf!"[27] in a way, offers a response to the question, what if there really was only one thing: do not answer!

Notes

1   Félix Guattari, *Parménide*, German trans. Iloe Ariss, from original transcription by Stéphane Nadaud, 2024. Transcript pages are noted below.

2   Martin Heidegger, *Gesamtausgabe*. 7: Vorträge und Aufsätze, "Das Ding," Frankfurt am Main: Klostermann, 2000, 175.

3   Plato, *The Collected Dialogues of Plato: Including the Letters*, "Parmenides," ed. Edith Hamilton, 16. Print, Bollingen Series 71, Princeton, NJ: Princeton University Press, 1996, 930, sn., 136a.

4   Guattari, *Parménide* trans. Ariss, 5.

5   Ibid.

6   Ibid.

7   Ibid., 6.

8   Ibid., 7.
9   Plato, *Parmenides*, 931, sn., 137c.
10 Ibid., 936, sn., 142c-d.
11 Guattari, *Parménide* trans. Ariss, 8.
12 Plato, *Parmenides*, 965, sn., 166b.
13 Guattari, *Parménide* trans. Ariss, 11–12.
14 Ibid., 12.
15 Heidegger, "Das Ding," 178.
16 Guattari, *Parménide* trans. Ariss, 11–12.
17 Ibid., 10.
18 Heidegger, "Das Ding," 179.
19 Ibid., 182.
20 Guattari, *Parménide* trans. Ariss, 6.
21 Plato, *Parmenides*, 932–5, sn., 137e–141e.
22 Ibid., 935, sn., 142a.
23 Guattari, *Parménide* trans. Ariss, 14.
24 Ibid., 15.
25 Martin Heidegger, *Gesamtausgabe*. 54: II. Abteilung: Vorlesungen 1923–1944, *Parmenides*, Frankfurt am Main: Klostermann, 2000, 175, 7.
26 Guattari, *Parménide* trans. Ariss, 13.
27 Ibid., 15.

References

Heidegger, Martin, *Gesamtausgabe,* Frankfurt am Main: Klostermann, 2000.
Plato, *The Collected Dialogues of Plato: Including the Letters*, ed. Edith Hamilton, 16. Print, Bollingen Series 71, Princeton, NJ: Princeton University Press, 1996.

12

Infernal Machines: The Guattaro-Witkacian Theatre of Theory

Benjamin Bandosz

Félix Guattari's philosophy casts a long shadow that obscures much of his artistic and creative output. His collaborative texts and his independently written work stand as significant contributions to Continental thought, psychoanalysis, semiotics, and critical theory. Throughout his theoretical work, he never fails to emphasize the philosophical core of art; whether Antonin Artaud's Body without Organs, the faciality of Japanese architecture, or the problematic refrains of Stanisław Witkiewicz's theater, Guattari views art as a potent vehicle for theory. It then comes as no surprise that Guattari's artistic works explore and embody his theories. We can count the fragment *cum* script, *Parmenides*, as one of these creative texts, whose brevity belies both its exploration of Guattarian concepts and its resonance with the avant-garde, Polish dramaturgy of Stanisław Ignancy Witkiewicz, better known as Witkacy. The Polish translation of *Parmenides* puts the kindred bond between Guattari and Witkacy's theories and dramaturgy into stark relief. This accompanying comparative analysis will examine the parallels between Witkacy's and Guattari's philosophical convictions to better map out the Witkacian topography of Guattari's fragment-script.

Guattari's analysis, creation, and production of theatrical work span across most of his intellectual and institutional life and work. In the first pages of *Anti-Oedipus*, Deleuze and Guattari use Antonin Artaud's notion of the Body without Organs from *To Be Done with the Judgment of God* to initiate their line of flight.[1] They use the Body without Organs as a theoretical model to explore a radical, alternative mode of being, experience, and, ultimately, becoming, that approaches the limits of signification and subjectification. Throughout his collaborative and independent texts, Guattari uses Artaud's concept to further his development and applications of schizoanalysis, though he does not limit himself to Artaud. Guattari develops and reworks notions like becoming, minor cinema, minor literature, ritornellos, semiotic black holes, and faciality through analyzing the works and lives of artists like Franz Kafka, Marcel Proust, Terrence Malick, and Claude Debussy. Inasmuch as schizoanalysis drew on and responded to the theoretical works of Freud, Jacques Lacan, Michel Foucault, Marx, and other strict discursive thinkers, Guattari regarded artistic works as containing richer theoretical and analytic dimensions. Indeed, in *Chaosmosis*, he emphasizes the analytico-philosophical potency of art: "If you want to analyze your unconscious [...] refer to the richest authors—Proust, Beckett, Joyce, Faulkner, Kafka or Artaud—because scarcely anything better has been done since."[2] Throughout his intellectual life, Guattari consistently uses creative works as exemplary renditions of his schizoanalytic theories. There is a lengthy catalog of artists Guattari draws on in his theoretical extrapolations. Witkacy is perhaps one of the few whose own philosophy resembles the schizoanalytic concepts Guattari uses to analyze his theatrical works.

Guattari's knowledge and appreciation of Witkacy are recorded in his short piece about the Polish polymath's play, *The Pragmatists*. In "Ethico-aesthetic Refrains in the Theatre of Witkiewicz," collected as an appendix in *Schizoanalytic Cartographies*,[3] Guattari uses Witkacy's play to explore the concept of problematic refrains, or abstract machines; that is to say, he sees how Witkacy uses "an aesthetic strategy of intensive repetitions" that violently ruptures representation and produces novel ontological coordinates.[4] This short, yet dense, piece on Witkacy has garnered little critical attention. Guattari's analysis and fascination with the play's disquieting absurdity betray a fixation on Wtikacy's dramaturgy that expresses the latter's own aesthetic and ontological theories. Indeed, at the end of the piece, Guattari begins to gain momentum by discussing *The Pragmatists* in relation to Witkacy's other pieces, *Gyubal Wahazar* and *The Water Hen*, noting a consistent use of concrete and abstract refrains in Witkacy's work. Michael Goddard notes how Witkacy's particular form of theater "constitutes for Guattari an exemplary case of an artistic schizoanalytic cartography."[5] In a certain sense, Goddard reduces Witkacy's play to a unidimensional text by labeling it as an "*artistic* schizoanalytic cartography." According to Witkacy, his plays, novels, and paintings are the media through which he expresses his philosophical theories. That is to say, what Guattari's reading of refrains registers is Witkacy's own theories of ontology and art.

The Pragmatists is one of Witkacy's initial attempts to theatrically express his theory of Pure Form. On December 29, 1921, Witkacy gave a lecture about his theory of Pure Form in Warsaw's Mały Theatre. Conceived by Witkacy while he was fighting in the eastern front's trenches during the First World War, the theory of Pure Form understands art as having an autonomous constructional function that instigates direct, undetermined affect rather than using established schemas of representation.[6] Witkacy argues for a nonrepresentational dramaturgy that embodies the metaphysical horror of existence—theater must strive to achieve an unmitigated relationality with life. Despite corresponding with Edmund Husserl, Roman Ingarden, Johannes Wilhelm Cornelius, and other interwar thinkers, Witkacy primarily examines and expresses his philosophical convictions in his plays and novels rather than treatises. For Witkiewicz, art is intimately bound up in ontology; thereby it synchronously describes and actualizes philosophical quandaries. It is not unsurprising, then, that Guattari was drawn to *The Pragmatists*, because it is Witkacy's "first play to illustrate his theory of Pure Form, according to which drama should be liberated from psychologically conceived characters and realistic storytelling."[7] The problematic refrains Guattari identifies in the play are instances of Witkacy's displays of Pure Form: ruptures with representation that attempt to grasp the forming, deforming, and un-forming of being. As Daniel Gerould points out, the play "presents an eternal moment into which all experience has been condensed."[8] Guattari identifies a potent theoretical core in *The Pragmatists*, which informs his schizoanalytic reading.

Witkacy's emphasis on the psychosomatic foundations of his ontological-metaphysical theories finds direct expression in

Guattari's theories and, by extension, his fragment-script *Parmenides*. Throughout the 1920s and 1930s, Witkacy further developed his philosophical system by predicating his ontology on a radical materiality that borrows from biology and physics. Witkacy describes his philosophical system as materialistic and biological, but avoids reductionism by insisting upon a complex ontological entanglement between different substances. Witkiewicz rejects Husserl's phenomenology, citing the latter's over reliance on visual and cognitive perception, which brackets the body from the experience of existence. For Witkacy, questions of perception and the knowledge of perception are ultimately ontological problems that are grounded in the holistic experience of existence—being conscious of something can be likened to having it melt into that which is bodily or perceived by the body, like ice cubes in water.[9] Witkiewicz's ontological system focuses on the self's unmediated relation to all other entities, all substances' molecular proximity and mutual entanglements make up what the playwright-philosopher understands as a bodily monism, or a monism of substance. This conception decentralizes the self, making it immanent rather than transcendental. This infinite proximity and seamless blending of consistencies between being, other, and material resonate with Guattari's logic of schizoanalysis.

Starting from his earliest works to those published posthumously, Guattari grounds his theories within a radical materiality. His notions continue the trajectory of Witkacy's ontology into postmodernist thought. In *The Anti-Oedipus Papers*, the schizoanalyst professes that in regard to modeling and analyzing the unconscious, "it's better to biologize things than to turn everything into linguistics."[10] Like Witkacy, Guattari avoids simplistic reductionism in this materialistic move by emphasizing the complex entanglement between language, the body, genetic code, molecular biology, and subjectivity. Inasmuch as Guattari emphasizes the "molecular-level physical-chemical processes intrinsic to organic life" in his understanding of pragmatic semiotics, his work is much more preoccupied with the ontological registers of these semiotic processes.[11] This is what leads him to the ontological pragmatics of schizoanalysis, which searches for free radical modes of existence, or singularities, and their existential contexts within auto-generative structures of power.[12] In this sense, Guattari's unorthodox ontological system accounts for the molecular connections between semiotics, the biological, and being—the abstract working in tandem with the concrete. One of the primary ways Guattari reconciles abstract being and concrete materiality is the refrain, which finds expression in *Parmenides*. Guattari and Witkacy's insistence on a base materiality in their complex ontologies signals a certain intellectual resonance. While the schizoanalyst's creative output pales in comparison to Witkiewicz's, there are several instances of Guattari's uses of literature to express his theoretical concepts.

Parmenides finds itself in a constellation of film and theater scripts that Guattari either wrote, worked on, or produced. As François Dosse notes, Guattari "tried his hand at every literary genre—poetry, novels, theater, scripts, memoirs, dreams."[13] One of these artistic ventures was a movie script. In the 1970s and 1980s, Guattari worked on a script with American director Robert Kramer. Eventually, Guattari finished the final draft of the script in 1987—it was titled *Un amour d'UIQ*, or *A Love of UIQ*. The script was a sci-fi, quasi-cyberpunk narrative about a squat community's communications with an infinitesimal alien, who later runs amok in the broader world with cataclysmic results. As I argue elsewhere, the script functions as an intermediary enunciation of Guattari's minor cinema and postmedia theories, reconfiguring the former into an initial formulation of the latter.[14] Though he would convince go-betweens to pass the script to directors like Francis Ford Coppola and Steven Spielberg, a proper film production never took shape.[15] That is not to say, however, that Guattari never realized any of his creative projects. At the private psychiatric clinic where he worked, La Borde, Guattari was the great organizer; he oversaw many workshops, committees, and projects involving staff, volunteers, and patients alike. One of the annual projects the patients and staff undertook was the production and performance of a play. La Borde's annual play was recorded by documentarian Nicholas Philibert in *La moindre des choses*. The documentary depicts how the staff and patients engage in the collective processes of producing and putting on a play, many of which Guattari would have facilitated throughout his career at La Borde. It is through such collaborative projects that Guattari both developed and applied his theories. For example, he undoubtedly saw the capacity of theater—and other forms of art—to generate transversal relations between staff and patients, or noticed the potentiality of a piece's or song's refrains to shift people out of their obsessional or paranoiac apprehensions. Though he only published one creative piece in his lifetime, *Ritournelle(s)*,[16] Guattari understood the valuable theoretical vehicle provided by literature. His fragment-script demonstrates another one of these literary attempts.

In *Parmenides*, a meandering and repetitive conversation between unknown parties slowly fractures the representational surface of the play. The refrains of interjections, questions, and clarifications, along with the sudden appearance of Juno—as though from an outside reality—which consumes the dialogue with her body, hearken to Witkiewicz's *The Pragmatists* and its various concrete refrains that find their problematic refrain in the apparatuses of artistic creation "threatened by the intrusion of the woman-mother as object of desire."[17] At the same time, the aimless conversation recalls Plasfodor's insistence of talking, any act of talking, to affirm existence itself.[18] There is a vertigo that exists between the unknown parties' lines of dialogue; not only is the discussion characterized by an amnesiac aphasia, the unmoored speaking subject floats in an existential void. Conversation, in this sense, is "the most significant way of experiencing life" for the unknown characters, and talking is what reaffirms existence in and of itself.[19] The repetition of the dialogue, especially with its return to the one thing (*jedna rzecz*), evokes the eternal return. By revisiting and rewording the same subject of "the one thing"—perhaps the primordial oneness and trying to think the beginning à la Heidegger's *Parmenides*—the conversation takes on a compulsive repetition that attempts to grasp its own meaning, only for it to lose the thread so it can try again.[20] As noted, the abrupt ending with the entrance of Juno recalls Guattari's reading of *The Pragmatists*. The Roman goddess of marriage and primordial mother, Juno, interjects—not unlike the verbal interjections—acting as a *coupure* to the existence-priming conversation of the unknown parties. The concrete refrains preoccupied with the primordial, Parmenidean oneness are reined in by the mystery of Juno, though the repetitive miscommunications do continue.

By linking Guattari's refrains and fragment to Witkacy's ontology and theater, we identify a philosophical consistency between the two playwrights and thinkers. In *The Pragmatists,* theater produces a different form of life rather than merely representing life, it "leads to an autopoietic account of theatre. It is this conception of theatre as a particular domain for the constitution of life."[21] That is, the various, concrete refrains found throughout the play—the verbal, the a-signifying, the colored and plastic, the gesticulative—function together to animate a problematic, or abstract, refrain that diffuses a mode of being which crosses the threshold of an obsessional or paranoid modality into a new ontological circumstance.[22] In *Parmenides,* we find a similar use of refrains that attempts to sustain an existence that continuously elides representation; it produces a primordial dimension by evoking a Parmenidean oneness through a compulsive repetition. Both Witkacy and Guattari recognize the capacity of art, be it theater, literature, or painting, to embody complex ontological theories and problems. What's more, they both give precedence to nonrepresentation in their work, acknowledging that the predetermined social, cognitive, and linguistic schemas contain existence and being within reductive categories. Through a radical ontology grounded in nondiscursive materiality, Witkacy and Guattari propose inventive modes of thinking, being, and art.

Notes

1 Deleuze and Guattari, *Anti-Oedipus: Capitalism and Schizophrenia,* trans. Robert Hurley et al, New York: Viking, 1977, 9ff.

2 Guattari, *Chaosmosis,* trans. Paul Bains and Julian Pefanis, Bloomington, IN: Indiana University Press, 1995, 182.

3   Guattari, "Ethico-Aesthetic Refrains in the Theatre of Witkiewicz," in *Schizoanalytic Cartographies*, trans. Andrew Goffey, London: Bloomsbury, 2013, 241–6.

4   Michael Goddard, "Diagram for a Transversal, Molecular Feminism? Guattari's Refrain and the Machinic-Feminine in Witkiewicz's The Pragmatists," *Women: A Cultural Review* 16/3 (2005): 275.

5   Goddard, "Diagram," 291.

6   Stanisław Ignacy Witkiewicz, *Seven Plays*, trans. Daniel Gerould, New York: Martin E. Segal Theatre Center Publications, 2004, 147.

7   Daniel Gerould, *Witkacy; Stanisław Ignacy Witkiewicz as an Imaginative Writer*, Seattle, WA: University of Washington Press, 1981, 64.

8   Ibid., 65.

9   Bohdan Michalski, *Metafizycy polskiej filozofii: Ingarden, Witkacy, Leszczyński: spór o istnienie świata realnego*, Warszawa: Wydawn. IFiSPAN / Collegium Civitas Press, 2002, 86, 100.

10 Guattari, *The Anti-Oedipus Papers*, trans. Kelina Gotman, New York: Semiotext(e), 2006, 75.

11 Janell Watson, *Guattari's Diagrammatic Thought: Writing between Lacan and Deleuze*, London: Continuum, 2009, 74.

12 Eugene B. Young, et al. *The Deleuze and Guattari Dictionary*, London: Bloomsbury, 2013, 271.

13 Francois Dosse, *Gilles Deleuze and Félix Guattari: Intersecting Lives*, trans. Deborah Glassman, New York: Columbia University Press, 2011, 428.

14 Benjamin Bandosz, "Potentialities of Post-Media: Networks of Resistance and Subjugation in Félix Guattari's *A Love of UIQ*," *Deleuze and Guattari Studies* 15/1 (2021): 119.

15 See Silvia Maglioni and Graeme Thomson, "UIQ: TOWARDS AN INFRAQUARK CINEMA (OR AN UNMAKING-OF)," in *A Love of UIQ*, trans. Silvia Maglioni and Graeme Thomson, Minneapolis, MN: Univocal, 2012, 13–48.

16 Guattari, *Ritournelles,* Tours: Lume, 2007.

17 Guattari, "Ethico-Aesthetic Refrains," 245.

18 Witkiewicz, *Seven Plays*, 28.

19 Ibid., 28.

20 Martin Heidegger, *Parmenides*, trans. Andre Schuwer and Richard Rojcewicz, Bloomington, IN: Indiana University Press, 1992, 7.

21 Goddard, "Diagram," 275.

22 Guattari, "Ethico-Aesthetic Refrains," 242–5.

References

Bandosz, Benjamin, "Potentialities of Post-Media: Networks of Resistance and Subjugation in Félix Guattari's *A Love of UIQ*," *Deleuze and Guattari Studies* 15/1 (2021): 117–39.

Dosse, Francois, *Gilles Deleuze and Félix Guattari: Intersecting Lives*, trans. Deborah Glassman, New York: Columbia University Press, 2011.

Gerould, Daniel, *Witkacy; Stanisław Ignacy Witkiewicz as an Imaginative Writer*, Seattle, WA: University of Washington Press, 1981.

Goddard, Michael, "Diagram for a Transversal, Molecular Feminism? Guattari's Refrain and the Machinic-Feminine in Witkiewicz's The Pragmatists," *Women: A Cultural Review* 16/3 (2005): 271–83.

Guattari, Félix, *Chaosmosis: An Ethico-Aesthetic Paradigm*, trans. Paul Bains and Julian Pefanis, Bloomington, IN: Indiana University Press, 1995.

Guattari, Félix, *The Anti-Oedipus Papers*, trans. Kelina Gotman, New York: Semiotext(e), 2006.

Guattari, Félix, *Schizoanalytic Cartographies*, trans. Andrew Goffey, London: Bloomsbury, 2013.

Heidegger, Martin, *Parmenides*, trans. Andre Schuwer and Richard Rojcewicz, Bloomington, IN: Indiana University Press, 1992.

Maglioni, Silvia, and Graeme Thomson, "UIQ: TOWARDS AN INFRAQUARK CINEMA (OR AN UNMAKING-OF)," *A Love of UIQ*, trans. Silvia Maglioni and Graeme Thomson, Minneapolis, MN: Univocal, 2012, 13–48.

Markowski, Michał Paweł, *Polska literatura nowoczesna: Leśian, Schulz, Witkacy*, Kraków: Universitas, 2007.

Michalski, Bohdan, *Metafizycy polskiej filozofii: Ingarden, Witkacy, Leszczyński: spór o istnienie świata realnego*, Warszawa: Wydawn. IFiSPAN / Collegium Civitas Press, 2002.

Watson, Janell, *Guattari's Diagrammatic Thought: Writing between Lacan and Deleuze*, London: Continuum, 2009.

Witkiewicz, Stanisław Ignacy. *Seven Plays*, trans. Daniel Gerould, New York: Martin E. Segal Theatre Center Publications, 2004.

Young, Eugene B., et al. *The Deleuze and Guattari Dictionary*, London: Bloomsbury, 2013.

PART THREE

REFERENCE TEXTS

13

Portrait of Félix Guattari as a Playwright

Flore Garcin-Marrou
Translated by Jay Hetrick

Félix Guattari was also a novelist, poet, playwright, and screenwriter, although these aspects of his work have been relatively overlooked. His formidable autobiographical account published, thanks to Jean-Baptiste Thierrée, as *Ritournelles* in 2007,[1] shows that over many years Guattari developed a surrealist style in the tradition of the Beat poets, giving life to a prose connected to his own stream of consciousness. It's now time to dive into the archives of the Félix Guattari collection, to take a studious seat in the nave of the Ardenne Abbey of the Institut Mémoire des Éditions Contemporaines (IMEC), and discover amongst other things the poetry collection *Crac en plan, pas un pli*, multiple versions of the screenplay *Un Amour d'UIQ*, as well as twelve plays composed between 1979 and 1990 that remain unpublished to this day.[2] *L'Affaire du sac de chez Lancel* (1979), *Le Maître de lune*, *Psyché Ville Morte*, *Socrates*, *Visa le noir tua le blanc* (1985–6), and *La*

Nuit, la fin des moyens (1990)—the six most accomplished of these plays—exist in multiple versions showing that they were reworked many times. During Guattari's lifetime, they circulated amongst his artist friends, prompting two sequels. *Socrates*, in a version reworked by Enzo Cormann, gave rise to a lecture-performance at the Théâtre Ouvert in Paris on January 18, 1988. *La Nuit, la fin des moyens* was performed at the Avignon Festival in 1990. But there are also less accomplished and undated dialogs (*Dialogue théâtral entre Toc, Tric et Mistrac, Dialogue théâtral entre Élodie, Robinson et Arsinoé, Dialogue entre Thérèse et Ugo*), plays inspired by Beckett (*Ding, Les Cubes*), as well as a Dadaist rewriting of a philosophical dialog (*Parménide*), the subject of this volume. Why did Guattari become so involved in playwriting? To what type of theater does his writing refer? Does he write, like Jean-Paul Sartre, a theater with a thesis that develops on stage the problems raised in his theoretical work? No, his theater goes in the opposite direction of this expectation because this comic, schoolboy, and dada-inspired theater testifies to an existential posture that the author has never ceased to claim: that of never being where one expects him to be, never inhabiting the center of things, but rather exploring the peripheries and margins. Aiming for theatrical writing is a way of reaching for other territories of experimentation, of becoming-nomad. If these plays have been overlooked and have not aroused much interest amongst directors, does this mean that they should be forgotten?

As a child, Guattari explains in *Ritournelles*, he attended matinee performances with his mother. He developed an almost fetishistic relationship with the theater programs, which he conscientiously kept in a drawer, to such an extent that his mother asked him if he preferred his collection of programs to the shows themselves. As a teenager—thanks to his friend Raymond Petit, organizer of cultural outings for the Groupe Jeunes de l'usine Hispano-Suiza de Bois-Colombes—Guattari took advantage of theater evenings organized for young workers. He then immersed himself in the writings of Sartre, his model of polygraphy, who was able to bring the philosophical and theatrical stages into dialog.

As early as 1953, when Guattari joined La Borde, he discovered a new type of theater connected to institutional psychotherapy. Thanks to François Tosquelles and the Saint-Alban experiment, intra-hospital clubs enabled occupational therapy workshops to be introduced. Then Jean Oury established the "theater function" at La Borde. For him, theater facilitates the formation of collectives, the decompartmentalization of the insane, and the creation of virtual spaces where psychiatry can experiment with a new distribution of roles. Some doctors play crazy, and crazy people play crazier than they actually are. New situational repertoires are put into place: the grid, a staging of everyday life, disallows any immobility. Those performing a role don't have the time to memorize it before it already must be altered: "Each morning, everything has to begin again."[3] Theater has become one of the clinic's emblematic therapeutic activities, most notably at the annual August 15 festival. There are also the "can-can marionettes"[4] who, every Saturday evening, comment on the week's activities: taking medication, clashes between doctors and patients. The puppets humorously give voice to what everyone is thinking about the institution.

A number of personalities visiting or residing at La Borde went there to write plays. At Jean Oury's invitation, Fernand Deligny staged a number of texts with the patients. Jacques Besse, musical director of the Charles Dullin company, established a reputation as the "Marquis de Sade of La Borde." Without turning the place into a new Charenton, Besse wrote a play that mobilized the enthusiasm of all those who lived and worked at the clinic. *Exotique Occident* praises the virtues of Professor Mac Bidaut, the mad inventor of a machine called the analitron: a strange device that sends out rays, which increase the intelligence of the average human and transform them into a genius. The operation is even more dangerous for a genius, whom it drives mad. Suspected of having sold the weapon to the Soviets, Mac Bidaut sinks into a depression that makes him "eat pineapples" and "drink liters." The show was performed in 1966 at the Palais de Tokyo, as part of Lacan's seminar, by patients and caregivers. Roland Dubillard, after frequenting La Borde, composed a sketch for the *Diablogues* called "Le Compte-gouttes," which was directly inspired by the place and its inhabitants, that features two residents trying to count all the drops in their glasses: "But how do you expect me to count the drops? You can't see them anymore!" Guattari surrounded himself with artists, often inviting them to work at La Borde. Dubillard was a member of the Groupe Théâtre de la FGERI. Jean-Jacques Lebel joined him at CERFI in order to open a new poetic and theatrical space, and introduced him to Judith Malina and Julian Beck from the Living Theatre during the events of May. Baptiste the magician, who later became the circus artist Jean-Baptiste Thierrée, came to run a year-long theater workshop in 1969. The residents gave several performances of a play by Jacques Sternberg, *C'est la guerre, monsieur Grüber*, at the Théâtre du Lucernaire. Guattari was increasingly attracted by the attempts of various artists to overturn established codes of representation, for example Jean-Baptiste Thierrée's work to revitalize the traditional circus and create the Nouveau Cirque. He was amazed by the modernity of Philip Glass and Bob Wilson's performance *Einstein on the Beach*. The same goes for Georges Aperghis' ATEM (Atelier théâtre et musique). Guattari made friends with his favorite actor, Jean-Pierre Léaud, and with Laura Betti who worked with Pasolini. In *Molecular Revolution*, he reviewed a show by a troupe called "Les Mirabelles," a collective of young members of the Front homosexuel d'action révolutionnaire (FHAR)—"happy drag queens," in his words—campaigning for the existence of a minority theater against the molar theater.[5]

In the early 1980s, during the "winter years" that marked the end of the experimental movements and creative utopias which animated the 1960s and 1970s, Félix Guattari began to write literature. While some may speak of a theoretical glaciation that reflects the malaise provoked by the completion of the joint project of *A Thousand Plateaus*, for Guattari these years signaled a real aesthetic shift. Between 1980 and 1986, he considered the idea of becoming a writer. In 1977, he began writing film scripts in response to the protests of the autonomist movements in Bologna. These literary experiments led him to think not only in terms of philosophical and clinical paradigms, but also in terms of aesthetics: "it is in underground art that we find some of the most important cells of resistance against the steamroller of capitalist subjectivity."[6] For a decade, it was art that kept him from succumbing to that glaciation. He championed Coluche, who embodies the artist that resists power. Coluche is the Shakespearean fool, the jester whose social function is to subvert values and conjure up new ones. In 1985, the director Philippe Adrien turned Guattari's manuscript of *Soixante-*

cinq rêves de Kafka into a performance entitled *Rêves de Kafka*.[7] With Jean-Jacques Lebel, Guattari created the Fondation Transculturelle Internationale. On several occasions, he was involved with and even performed at the Polyphonix sound poetry festival. Alone and with Joël Hubaut, he passed through the looking glass, took to the stage, and unraveled the thread of his thoughts in self-schizoanalysis: a letting go in speech and writing, which he then committed to paper.

Of the twelve existing plays, I would like to bring attention to four pieces. The first, in the spirit of the October Group and agitprop plays, shows how theater can stage the political. *L'Affaire du sac de chez Lancel* is a militant play written in 1979, inspired by a real incident. During a demonstration by metal workers, Guattari's friend, director François Pain, was photographed as he appeared to grab a handbag from the vitrine of a Lancel shop near the Place de l'Opéra. The photograph made the front page of the far-right newspaper *Minute* the following day and was used by police to arrest Pain and bring him to trial. In protest, Guattari wrote a "courtroom burlesque" denouncing the absurdity of the legal system. At the end of the play, the judge yields to public protest and the entire room breaks into a farandole.

The second piece, *Le Maître de lune* (1984), allows us to see and hear mental confusion, a chaotic imaginary expressed in the language of the characters as well as the constitution of their bodies. It is a "chaosmic sketch" that Guattari hoped to be directed by Philippe Adrien, set to music by Enzo Cormann, choreographed by Daniel Dobbels, and set-designed by Gérard Fromanger. The play recounts the impossible union of Sun and Moon, masculine and feminine. In the course of the plot, the moon takes over the sun, transforms into a capitalist sphinx, and then becomes a robot. The twelve actors wear unisex costumes, which they alter and paint themselves during the performance in a practice akin to body art. The notations (A, B, C) are reminiscent of Beckett. The whole thing resembles a happening, an open work—as theorized by Umberto Eco—a massive work in progress inspired by the writing of the Beat Generation. Guattari, like Allen Ginsberg, connects directly to unconscious flow. The piece is a palimpsest of writing, a patchwork of childish ritornellos ("Ja/Ja/ cr'sshair,/Jojo/The louse/King of the fartsoolies"), epic lines ("Under a sky of heavy tears, Lady Tartine, Queen of the Styx, empties her soul"), and dreamlike expressions ("As soon as I saw her, an iguana dream landed on the back of my neck").[8] It bears witness to a desire to create amphigoric theater.

Le Maître de lune has a few themes in common with the third piece, *Visa le noir tua le blanc*, which was probably written between 1985 and 1987. The title evokes the lyrics of the traditional French song "V'la l'bon vent," which recounts the story of a king's son who, while passing by a pond, took aim at a black duck but ended up killing a white one. The play transports us to childhood and provides a theatrical reflection on the concept of the ritornello. The nine anonymous actors have no names, but are rather identified by letters, from A to I. These characters are accompanied by a machine, a voiceover, a Christ Pantocrator who appears in a holographic projection, as well as Comte West West and his hunting instructor. Some of the characters designated by letters are followed by a "processional chain of doubles,"[9] held together at a distance of six meters with an invisible thread. A, B, C, and D don't appear to be humans, but rather abstract signs forming a signifying chain, as Jacques Lacan might have formulated it: letters which, when assembled, form words and sentences in the subject's unconscious.

Guattari is criticizing the structuralist conception of the disappearance of the subject, where the human can only be apprehended through a network of symbolic relations within a structure in which it blindly participates, thereby substituting the impersonal necessity of the system for the freedom of the subject. The theatrical characters reflect this idea since they are not portrayed as individuals, but as letters that are linked together to create a structure. But the uniqueness of *Visa le noir tua le blanc* also lies in its interrogation of the origin of things. The characters on stage are distraught, attempting to make some connection. One wonders: has anything ever happened? Why is there something rather than nothing? Such questions, inherited from the philosophy of Leibniz, set the stage for characters in search of action (here, too, we detect a Pirandellian resonance). The play is concerned with drama and its obstacles. In his *Poetics*, Aristotle defines theater in terms of a narrative that develops from point A to point B. Guattari rejects this dramatic principle since, in this play, nothing happens. As in Samuel Beckett's theater—most notably, *Waiting for Godot* and *Endgame*—the characters are simply waiting for something that never transpires. But are they even waiting? Structuralism seems to devalue the event or phenomenon in favor of structure and it seems to be this tension that the characters experience. But to this dramatic crisis, the character labeled N proposes a solution. Then G protests: "This one's going to do the clinamen trick again."[10] The clinamen appears here as a new dramatic principle. Attributed to Epicurus and developed by Lucretius, it refers to the deviation of atoms as they fall vertically in the void. Atoms deviate, collide, and thereby enable everything to exist. Metaphorically speaking, the characters represent atoms that are free to move in any direction. An actor gives birth to an event, a story, a drama when they encounter another character and establish a dialog. The clinamen triggers a reflection on the actor's craft, toward a conception of the stage as a particle accelerator, and a principle of dramatic writing that formally opposes all determinism. Used by Pataphysics and Oulipo, this approach allows us to envisage writing as the search for chance collisions, deviating from the constraints of language and syntax in order to create distortions, outbursts of freedom, and new forms of play.

Similar themes are taken up in Félix Guattari's last and most accomplished play, *La Nuit, la fin des moyens*, written in 1990. A one-off performance took place at the Avignon Festival, which was completely unnoticed by the regional and national press. This ninety-page piece, subtitled "Palimpsest for the theatre," turns out to be a theatrical rewriting of his autobiographical work *Ritournelles*. The literary object has been cut up and sewn back together from a multitude of textual fragments from notebooks and diaries. It is an unidentified theatrical object with no apparent narrative thread that leads the spectator from point A to point B. There might not even be a plot, but only aborted situations and characters in search of an author who languish in situations they are unable to create. Once again, the play is concerned with the obstruction or prevention of drama itself. Rather than following a traditional narrative structure ("once upon a time ... "), Guattari aims to deconstruct drama only to reconstruct it differently. In the same way that Samuel Beckett's *Watt* is an attempt to write a novel without a plot, this play is truly an "a-dramatic" drama. Midori is a young Japanese woman. From the outset, she appears frozen in a red gelatinous mass mirroring Ralph, the militant communist, who is frozen in a blue gelatinous mass. She meditates on chaos, the stage, the meaning of everything. He often performs short passages from *Ritournelles*, enunciating snippets of autobiographical memories that punctuate the situation with flashes of light and images. She appears draped in a black cape with fur and black straps, passing through customs at JFK Airport in New York. He sometimes recites, in full, paragraph 279 of Book IV of Nietzsche's *Daybreak*. Like a puppet, she obeys the commands of a third character named Collor, a Brazilian in his forties. He also has trouble finding his true identity, a fragmented body who struggles to grasp its unity. Collor has Midori and Ralph under his control. He has the power to immobilize them, just as he has the power to grant the "choir of yellow dogs" the status of characters. And the canine chorus does not fail to claim: "You are supposed to represent us, to bring us into existence, to speak in our name."[11] Collor is a *mise en abyme* of the playwright himself who, according to the principle of automatic writing, decides which action will unfold the minute it's written. "It the moment I'm writing, I'm totally unaware of what might happen," remarks Collor/ Guattari, adopting a form of aleatory writing. As in *Visa le noir tua le blanc*, Guattari problematizes the foundation of theater as the site of represented action (Aristotelian *mimesis praxeos*): why does something happen, rather than nothing? What happens in theater when nothing happens? Who has the power to make it happen?

To take this one step further, we can interpret *La Nuit, la fin des moyens* as a practical experiment in the "method of dramatization," as conceived by Gilles Deleuze in a 1967 article and later in *Difference and Repetition*.[12] Deleuze situates us within a little theater of the idea and demonstrates how, when we think, an idea emerges. First, it is a larva that differentiates by acquiring spatiotemporal coordinates when it emerges on a plane of immanence. It is then animated by speeds and rhythms. The idea is lived as an event that arises in thought and constitutes the veritable "drama of the thinker." Félix Guattari proceeds by analogy: in *La Nuit* the idea is the end of means, which is represented by the characters trapped within indistinct gelatinous masses, literally embodying larvae that have not yet been given a quality, a name, a face. We have Ralph and Midori—larval and gelatinized—on the plane of immanence (the theater stage), who are then assigned spatiotemporal positions, speeds of movement, and rhythms of diction as Collor/Guattari conceives his drama. In the same way that the method of dramatization allows us to understand the development of a larval state into an idea, *La Nuit, la fin des moyens* enables us to follow Ralph and Midori on the path of their constitution as characters. Dramatization, as Guattari experiments with it here, consists of the larval entity becoming a character, then the character appearing on stage and creating an event. This is analogous to philosophy, where dramatization involves a larval idea becoming an idea that manifests upon the stage of thought. The beginning of the play is "mired in the coagulations of meaning" enveloping the characters like an "icy mist." Collor senses the "danger of freezing," the "danger of the flight of ideas and logomachy," "an inescapable ordeal for apprehending multiple components at the intersection of which a scene and an event crystallizes." In order to become characters, the larvae must free themselves from their gelatinous masses and, to do so, must "delimit" and "demarcate" themselves by differentiating, first by a "division of sex," then according to a "division of age."[13] Ralph and Midori undergo the processes of differenciation on stage. The delimitation of these characters is also based on cellular division. Guattari speaks of "scissiparity," just as Deleuze literally evokes the division of the egg. The metamorphosis of entities into characters is gradual: "The contours of the characters are always shifting and the scene itself struggles to materialize. Nomadic flows envelop, bewitch, and conjure up a zone in-between two deaths: that of the collapse of narrative discourse and that which marks being with its seal of finitude."[14] After a few pages in which no situation manages to crystallize, a blue vapor invades the scene, provoking Ralph and Midori to withdraw into their original gelatinous masses. Collor does not want to witness his entities, his "larvae," transform into characters. On the contrary, he tries to preserve them as larval subjects: "Ralph, don't go away, don't lose your contour. A character normally takes shape through action and suspense. Nothing of the sort here, since the aim is to deconstruct significant compositions as they arise and, to this end, to retain a few of them in an almost aleatory manner."[15]

Guattari attempts to create a theater of obstruction: "For once, something was beginning to happen that concerned us all! … We stockpiled all kinds of machines to break, shatter, fragment, erase, to palimpsest the ebb and flow of subjectivity, with the ulterior motive that something would always come out of it."[16] Through Collor, Guattari experiments with an aleatory, immanent, and a-dramatic theatrical writing composed of heterogeneous fragments that point toward a theater yet to be invented. At the end of the play, Ralph describes this as a "theatre of the line of flight": "Lines, always lines … A flight, an implosion. Mimetics of oblivion and perpetual evasion."[17]

The object of this theater is no longer drama, but the process of writing itself. In this way, we can appreciate how Guattari belongs to a post-Beckettian lineage of dramaturgy that never ceases to question the dramatic act as such, a problem shared by playwrights of the late twentieth and early twenty-first centuries.

It is certainly too early to overlook the theater of Félix Guattari. His plays can stimulate not only an assemblage of specialists and academics who would view them for their historical value like objects in a museum. *La Nuit, la fin des moyens*, in particular, presents itself today as a play with a different scope and ambition in which Guattari develops—through the play of montage, the articulation of word and image, and the search for a becoming-stage—a veritable dramatic writing all his own.[18]

Notes

1 Félix Guattari, *Ritournelles*, Tours: Lume, 2007.

2 *Socrates* was the first piece to be published, in the issue of *Deleuze and Guattari Studies* dedicated to the twentieth anniversary of Guattari's death (Guattari 2012). It was translated by Solène Nicolas and introduced by me.

3 Jean-Claude Polack and Danielle Sivadon, *La Borde ou le droit à la folie*, Paris: Calmann-Lévy, 1976.

4 Jean Oury, "La désaliénation en clinique psychiatrique," *Présences* 54 (1956). Reprinted in Jean Oury, *Psychiatrie et psychothérapie institutionnelle*, Paris: Payot, 1977, 23–34.

5 Félix Guattari, "I Have Even Met Happy Drag Queens," trans. Rachel McComas, in *Soft Subversions*, ed. Sylvère Lotringer, New York: Semiotext(e), 1995, 37–9.

6   Félix Guattari, *Chaosmosis*, trans. Paul Bains and Julian Pefanis, Bloomington, IN: Indiana University Press, 1995, 91.

7   Félix Guattari, *Soixante-cinq rêves de Franz Kafka et autres textes,* Paris: Lignes, 2007.

8   Félix Guattari, *Le Maître de lune* (unpublished). © Bruno, Emmanuelle, and Stephen Guattari, Fonds IMEC.

9   Félix Guattari, *Visa le noir tua le blanc* (unpublished). © Bruno, Emmanuelle, and Stephen Guattari, Fonds IMEC.

10 Ibid.

11 Félix Guattari, *La Nuit, la fin des moyens* (unpublished). © Bruno, Emmanuelle, and Stephen Guattari, Fonds IMEC.

12 Gilles Deleuze, "The Method of Dramatization," in *Desert Islands and Other Texts,* ed. David Lapoujade, New York: Semiotext(e), 2004, 94–116.

13 Guattari, *La Nuit, la fin des moyens.*

14 Ibid.

15 Ibid.

16 Ibid.

17 Ibid.

18 For a more detailed discussion, see Flore Garcin-Marrou, "Gilles Deleuze, Félix Guattari: entre théâtre et philosophie. Pour un théâtre de l'à venir." PhD dissertation (French Literature, supervised by Denis Guénoun), Paris-Sorbonne University, 2011.

References

Deleuze, Gilles, "The Method of Dramatization," in *Desert Islands and Other Texts*, ed. David Lapoujade, New York: Semiotext(e), 2004, 94–116.

Guattari, Félix, *La Nuit, la fin des moyens* (unpublished). © Bruno, Emmanuelle, and Stephen Guattari, Fonds IMEC.

Guattari, Félix, *Le Maître de lune* (unpublished). © Bruno, Emmanuelle, and Stephen Guattari, Fonds IMEC.

Guattari, Félix, *Visa le noir tua le blanc* (unpublished). © Bruno, Emmanuelle, and Stephen Guattari, Fonds IMEC.
Guattari, Félix, "I Have Even Met Happy Drag Queens," trans. Rachel McComas, in *Soft Subversions*, ed. Sylvère Lotringer, New York: Semiotext(e), 1995, 37–9.
Guattari, Félix, *Chaosmosis*, trans. Paul Bains and Julian Pefanis, Bloomington, IN: Indiana University Press, 1995.
Guattari, Félix, *Ritournelles*, Tours: Lume, 2007.
Guattari, Félix, *Soixante-cinq rêves de Franz Kafka et autres textes*, Paris: Lignes, 2007.
Guattari, Félix, "Socrates," trans. Solène Nicolas, *Deleuze and Guattari Studies* 6/2 (2012), 173–86.
Oury, Jean, *Psychiatrie et psychothérapie institutionnelle*, Paris: Payot, 1977, 23–34.
Polack, Jean-Claude, and Danielle Sivadon, *La Borde ou le droit à la folie*, Paris: Calmann-Lévy, 1976.

14

Socrates

Félix Guattari
Translated by Solène Nicolas,
Arranged by Flore Garcin-Marrou

In a shadowy light.

Georges: I am Socrates.

Carmen: Now, now, here he goes again!

Georges: What? What's wrong with this? I am Socrates, big deal! There's no need to make a mountain out of it! *He goes near Carmen and starts talking with a Russian accent*: What is it, my Karmen, my candy Karma?

Carmen: It's ok, drop it!

Georges: Would She rather be my Catholic Caramel?

Carmen: Stop it, you're a real pain!

Georges: Notwithstanding, could I have the great good fortune and privilege to have a conversation with Her about a question that I dare describe as being in our common interest?

English translation of *Socrate* by Solène Nicolas, arranged by Flore Garcin-Marrou. © Bruno, Emmanuelle, Stephen Guattari, Fonds Guattari, IMEC.

Challenger: Can't you see she just answered: not now!

Georges: Could I be a-dreaming? Or could it be that someone just had the nerve to talk to me instead of her? Stand back, turkey turnkey!

Carmen: Will you please stop your act! Come on then, come **here**: what was it you wanted to tell me? *She beckons Challenger to walk away.* Challenger, you will give us some space for a minute, won't you? *To Georges*: And don't you take advantage of the situation. And try to understand this is the last time.

Georges: The very last one! Damn! If that is so, I will relinquish it for good then and might come to wearing my heart on my sleeve and having death on my banner. Surely you expected this to happen, my darling chimera: I'm not really the half-hearted kind. Shit, I'm a proud man after all!

Carmen: *Threatening*: Shut it! Come here, and come here quick. *Georges moves near her, scared, with bulging eyes.*

Georges: But I haven't done anything wrong!

Carmen: Come on, what is it you wanted to say?

Georges: Don't you worry! It's nothing really. For one thing, I've **already told you.**

Carmen: What? That you're Socrates? *He nods pitifully.*

Carmen: *To Challenger, who is still within earshot, though with his back turned*: Did you hear him this time? See, it's all starting up again. *An increasingly loud droning of planes can be heard. It is reminiscent of the bombers of the previous world war.*

Challenger: *Sidles up to Georges in a friendly way.* Are you at least **positive about this?** *Georges points to the sky.*

Challenger: Yes, I know that it's the Americans, but we should not worry too much about it!

Georges: It sounds more like military sedition to me.

Challenger: Forget about it. I'd rather hear about how it all came back.

Georges: *Casually.* How what came back? My being ... Socrates? Oh, that's easy enough. First there was like the striking of a match that is being broken in the middle, except that this time there was also the empty shape of sound—does that make any sense to you? So tell me, you really think that there is going to be war again?

Challenger: Maybe you haven't counted properly?

Carmen: How many weeks late?

Georges: I don't really know, it's difficult to say. But what I know for sure is that all the tests are positive.

Carmen: Surely you should have taken precautions.

...

Alphonse: *Greeting Carmen ceremoniously.* Do you know, fair lady, that this could be a massive breakthrough!

Challenger: What's-that-you-say?

Alphonse: My heartiest apologies, ladies and gentlemen, for interrupting your conversation. But when I saw what was brewing, it came as a shock and I said to myself, dear old Alphonse, surely the time has come ...

Challenger: What's that intrusive one going on about?

Alphonse: In my defence, you cannot ignore that in case of *force majeure*, they'll discard you as vain and smug if you don't have a stooge, but if there's two, or three, or four, or plenty of you, then no one will question your words. Therefore, bear with me, though I do not have the honour of a formal agreement, things can go smoothly ...

Challenger: That's what you say!

Carmen: But Mister ... what's your name again?

Alphonse: Alphonse, from Belgium.

Carmen: Dear Alphonse, since Alphonse you are, what have you inferred from your first approach to the problem?

Alphonse: The truth is, little more than the common folk, except that in this type of case one is entitled to expect additional information ....

Challenger: *That's* what I was expecting.

Carmen: Information about what, if you please?

Alphonse: *Doubtfully*. Something like a spiritual increase, a right to follow, a guarantee that it'll work or die ....

Carmen: Couldn't you be any more explicit?

Alphonse: Oh, but what do I know? Something that'd say he is mortal ....

Carmen: Quite a vague thing to say!

Alphonse: Or that he is a man ...

Challenger: I can't see any connection here!

They say the final lines from the top of their voices: the droning of the planes, which had at first decreased, gets louder and louder until it completely covers the voices. All the characters eventually flee from the explosion of bombs, leaving no one on the stage but Georges.

• • •

Georges walks to and fro.

Georges: In the shell of anguish A voiceless

>   So Soundless
>
>   Sound
>
>   Stone-deaf
>
>   Signifier signifying little
>
>   Beginning of something new …

An extremely tall postman who is very busy deciphering the address on a parcel, walks past without seeing him.

Postman: I say, this thing here is absolutely illegible.

>   BER … MACR … ARBEIT …

Georges: *He walks up to him*: May I?

Postman: Who are you?

Georges: Me? Hem … Let's say I'm Socrates.

Postman: Wait a minute … That doesn't look right. That's pushing it a bit! What with our poor wages! By the way, your thing, how do you spell it?

Georges: What? Socrates? The way it is pronounced: S for Socrates, O for Octavian, C for Caligula … But let me have a look …

Carmen: *Interrupting*: Don't give it to him! Don't you give it to him!

The postman raises his arms, holding the packet really high, so that none of them can reach it.

Postman: God! Make up your minds!

Carmen: But I'm telling you he's not the one!

Postman: *Showing the parcel.* But then, this thing here, who'd that be destined for? *Showing Carmen.* And that whirligig there, where does she come from?

Georges: You might call her my wife.

Postman: Good heavens! That's the story of my life, when there's too many things and too many people, I get mixed up.

Carmen: Stop the chatting, give that to me now.

She grabs the postman by the sleeve and tries to grab to parcel.

Postman: Ouch! Mrs. Socrates, have mercy! I happen to be extremely ticklish! No! Anything but that! Stop it or I'll call for help! Help! Someone help me!

Challenger walks in.

Challenger: Hey! You weirdos! What's the racket all about?
Postman: It's because of the Socrateses, Sir, they keep pestering me while I'm on duty.
Challenger: But you're mistaken, my dear friend! These people have nothing to do with Socrates!
Postman: Ah! Teach me something! It's my lucky day! But then … But then …

He scrutinizes the label on the parcel again.

Postman: Heavens! It does look like this is the name that's written there.
Georges: *Shouting in triumph*: Ah Ah! Of course! Zounds! I told you! Who was right? And how much had we bet on this?
Challenger: Be that as it may, Mister postman, rest assured that your man is not here.
Georges: Stop there! It's postmarked isn't it? What do you make of that? Where does it come from? Check the postmark! *Georges starts jumping in the air again to try and grab the parcel.* The postmark! The postmark! We want the postmark! I'm a taxpayer, I am! And I am entitled to read the postmark …

Carmen: *Reproachfully.* See the state he's in because of you!

Postman: Calm down, my friend. Wait, we'll check that together. It seems indeed to be a foreign stamp. *He shows the postmark to Georges who is standing on the tips of his toes.* There, you read it, for I haven't got the right glasses.

Georges deciphers the postmark painfully.

Georges: D ... E ... L ... Deli.

Challenger: New Delhi?

Postman: I'd rather expect something like Delicatessen.

Challenger: In that case, you could have Delfzije, Maigret's hometown.

Postman: No, it's De ... li ... gny. Or maybe: Del ... phoï. Yes, that right: Del ... phi. Delphi, in Phocis, on the hills of Montparnasse. Ah! Hometown! Home sweet home! Benzaï! Benzaï!

He catches the postman unawares, snatches the parcel out of his hands and flies away with it.

Postman: Wait! Wait and see! Per favor, Sir Socrates! You could at least sign the receipt for me!

Upset, he turns towards Carmen and holds out his ball point pen to her.

Postman: You, Mrs Socrates, you're the last reasonable person on this planet! You ain't gonna let me down, are you? You're gonna sign my receipt for me, aren't you?

Carmen walks away with a shrug of her shoulders as the poor postman falls on his knees, his arms still outstretched in her direction.

Postman: *Facing the public*: It's no wonder, in front of such ungratefulness, that the tricuspid valves of a man end up falling apart. Oh! I know that quite a few of us would have equally overlooked such an apparently futile stumbling of the symbol. Nothing to write home about, nothing to upset the original cosmic soup. Ok! I grant you that! Except that this comes as an echo to the cracking of the match that was previously pinpointed by our dear Georges, so don't we have ground to fear for the worst now: a general tumbling down of the dominos, a thorough and rolling disorder of all sports! But let's not procrastinate any longer, and let's now hunt for our unfortunate friend. …

Georges, holding the parcel in one hand and a bike in the other, is walking deeper into the ice flow.

Georges: They wouldn't have treated me any worse than this if I had robbed the key to the wind and rain!

Challenger's indistinct talking in the distance.

Georges: Goodbye! Vain mobs! Watch as I'll go and vanish into the chasm.

Challenger: Georges! Don't screw things up! Wait for me!

Challenger trips over a tree stump and falls down into a pond.

Challenger: OUCha! Somebody help me! Georges, can't you see I'm burning?

The head of Georges comes out of a burning bush on the tundra which is standing, as though on purpose, right next to Challenger.

Georges: Who art thou? Who comes hither and dares interrupt my celestial journey?

Challenger: But Georges! Don't you recognize me? Georges, Mister.

Georges!: It's me, Challenger, your faithful adversary.

Georges: *Raising his arms in the air*: Ah, dear Mister Challenger! What a surprise! And how is war developing? And how is our Lady-Wet-Blanket doing?

Challenger: You must be referring to Mrs Carmen? Well, she is as good as can be really. By the way, she insisted that I bring you back home *presto*.

Georges: Well, there, sweet companion ... for the time being, I am far from being done with all the life that's going on here. *He holds out the parcel.*

Challenger: What! You still haven't opened it?

Georges: It takes a fair amount of caution, if I may say so. And in those days ....Challenger: Do you fear something like a parcel bomb?

Georges: Please! Don't make me say things that you wouldn't want anyone else to have hushed from you! And do mark that I leave you with the entire responsibility of your assumptions. For, the truth is ... I have been through so many tropical torpors,

    Brain horrors

    Semantic storms

    Used so many verbs in the spring of the future

    In the present of the summer

    In the imperative of the winter,

    In the imperative of the autumn.

    I have been through red fire,

    I have swallowed purple pills,

> I have chewed some …
> What's their name again, those flowers with orange bells, as crispy as pizza crusts?

Challenger: Hem!

Georges: *With a motion of his mouth*. Ok then. May the bubbling torrents of octopus ideas and one-eyed algae that stew in my heart of hearts overflow and cover all things. But, enough emotion, tender Challenger, I've had enough of your standing here, sheepishly listening to me, you drive me nuts and bolts.

He holds out a huge gun and starts firing in the air.

Georges: Away you go, villain! Or it will be the end of you. Let's go! A fair amount of soup and to bed! And give the certified copy of my feelings to Carmen loud and clear.

Challenger: Precisely, she had thoroughly insisted that I ….

Gunshots again, this time aiming at Challenger's legs.

Georges: We know your tricks, you scoundrel!

Challenger: The bugger is going for my legs! Me, a mere messenger. Have mercy, mercy sir, have mercy.

Georges: *Derisively*. Mercysir! Mercy sir who?

Challenger: *With a ceremonious bow*: With your permission, I figure ….

Georges: There ain't no father figure or mother figure anymore, not as long you haven't poured your heart out, my good man. So, back to steerage. And first, port. What can you see?

Challenger: From port, I see the tundra's heart beating wildly. I see the chamois on the top and brim of laws, I see the gossamer sparrow and the tarantella mozzarella, I see ….

Georges: Here, right in front of you! Damn! Right here—*he points to himself*—what is there that you can see?

Challenger: Hem!

Georges: Avanti, popolo!

Challenger: What I see here, Master? But with no hesitation and no stooge, I see you, quite simply you, in your unflinching splendour, both unmatched and unequalled.

Georges: Isn't that just great? Pure wool! And with a handsome model, I grant you that. But me who what?

Challenger: *Aside.* The bugger! He's trying to trap me!

Georges: Come, speak boldly, regardless of my opinion and if you have something better to say, you'll have my blessing, I promise. I wouldn't be so surprised if your views turned out to be better than mine, for you seem to have studied these questions and learnt from the lessons of the other.

Challenger: When the salting came

    Salazar

    Went to meet

    With Balthazar

    Hola, Caesar! ...

Georges: You're evading my questions, you fool! Will you answer? Am I, or am I not the ultimate destination of this parcel? And there's no room for any mistaking, for you could *presto* become the final destination of the present bullet.

Showing his pistol.

Countdown: 7, 5, 14, 8, 3, 2 ...

The bombing starts again.

Challenger: That's it! You're Socrates! Have it your way, scum!

Georges: I didn't quite hear you, say it again. And double-quick or I'll blow your brains out!

There is some shy knocking at the door, which is soon followed by various sounds of pipes coming from the opposite wall. This gives way to new, louder sounds from the ceiling. It all combines to form a kind of symphony. Georges stands up cautiously and goes to look through the keyhole. He turns the lock as noiselessly as possible and comes back to his seat.

Georges: *Whispering.* At first, I hadn't taken it really seriously. Those things, you think that it will always be soon enough to think them through again. Moreover, in those days, I was still chased by that pack of children who cried out to me, from morning to night: 'Hola! Father Hemlock, aren't you going to open your parcel?' So I would turn around, good-humouredly, and threaten them: 'Just you wait, scoundrels, wait until I catch one of you!' They went and came like a flock of robins. But the day when there was no one and nothing ….

Scratching at the door.

Carmen: *With a plaintive voice.* Open, I beg you. Open, I know you're in there!

The phone rings. Georges's gaze goes from the door to the phone that is on the floor, and back again. He tiptoes his way to the phone, lifts up the receiver and puts it down without bothering to listen to it.

Georges: It feels like it's all starting up again!

Crystal clear voices seem to be raining from different sides:

Chorus: A B C D time has come … when time's up … it's not time … when time's up.

Multiple voices: Daglock, clock, knock, flock, lovelock, hemlock, wedlock, unlock, Sherlock …

Georges: Where was I? Yes, at first, I always came back without frowning to the cracking that they would later describe as essential:
CRACK
DIMENSION
NO HESITATION
This is all very nice, but, then, you're kind of stuck there. And meanwhile, I heard the echo of the nagging nag of the poor postman's despair or, to put it differently, it was like the bursting of all possible factorial analysis, what others had hurriedly linked to the fall from the post horse, which is famously crucial in the monograph of 'Little Hans'.

Someone kicks in the door. Georges leans against it to prevent it from being destroyed.

Carmen: Georges! Georges darling! Open to your Candy.

Carmen: Come back to me, don't leave me! You'll be my Socrates for life and I'll be your tarantella for the weekends. And every now and then, I swear to you, I'll hallow thy name, oh, my Socrates! The only object of my impact!

She puts her ear to the door, as Georges starts whispering again.

Georges: Apparently, nothing proves that this is actually hemlock. There's no tag on it, after all! Let's suppose it is though, we can't be sure that the bloody parcel was really addressed to me *in vino veritas*. We can't be sure that Postman Lanky wasn't the king of cheats and, supposing, just supposing, that the name here on the label is indeed Socrates, we still have to prove with no manipulation whatsoever that the applicant is indeed *recto verso* the one that's here talking to you Ladies and Gentlemen, and moreover that he-had-always-been-that, that is, that he was a man, and to top it off, that he was mortal and all that comes with that. Therefore, during that time, you must realize that ... (*He gives the finger*) I'm taking to my heels! Especially since we've left aside the question of whether it is possible to be a man without being mortal and *vice versa*, to be mortal without being a man, which is a lot less economical, I grant it, but there's no avoiding that you'll always have variations galore, all you can eat, and even, in the most extreme cases, it would have been seriously wise to actually give me some hemlock, but we should have checked in good time: PRIMO that it was *safo*, of the *Conium maculatum* type, not *Aethusa cynapium* or dog parsley, or sweet-and-sour-to-wash-it-down and, SECUNDO, that I hadn't myself been mithridatparalized in my suckling days or by a habit contracted while ambling around the world. And if they relentlessly told me that I moaned so much about the soup that someone would eventually think something about myself, vergogno! I would say to them, *in vitro* and *in peto*, that even facing them and without hindsight I would always have the liberty to come back to the shortest way, that is, speaking from a phenomenological point of view: what is that little thing our lives come down to? A something *outside* surrounded by a certain quantity of something *inside*. Presumably! Or if you'd rather, an outward doubled with some kind of interiority. That's not bad, boy! It has the same hard-on as Archimedes's lever. From then on, you can gather the ins and outs of why I fell pregnant. For, beware, my friends, no one ever speaks about that thing here! It has become, sort of, one two three, Totem and Taboo. But let us just suppose—a simple supposition, that we tie it back to that story, a medley of a story, with a clown's knickers and with my sister who has a bun in the oven! Mehr licht! Yet another bountiful idea! They give you three caskets: that of the body-jug to pour life (*he puts his hand on his stomach*), that of the gloom-room that is besieged by that mad woman (*he points to the door behind which Carmen is still restless*) and that of the hemlock to see the spry old birds through (*he pretends to drink a cup*). Alleluia, come down Yahweh! Bring down dawn and some phylum to unfreeze what's coming next …

The ceiling tumbles down under the weight of Challenger who is dressed up as an American soldier. The strings of his parachute keep him hanging in the air.

Georges: Oh my! You again!
    From outside: What's the matter with you my angel?
Carmen: You're not hurt, are you? Would you like me to call the firemen?
Challenger: *Telling him not to reveal anything with his forefinger on his mouth*. Hush. *He now points to his ears*: Mission Alcibiades: I have come incognito.

Georges: *Turning in Carmen's direction*: Don't you worry, ginger, everything's ok.

Georges climbs on a chair to try and take Challenger off his hook but the latter pushes him away.

Challenger: Let me do this, it's a rising model.

Challenger now shows what he meant and uses a remote control to go up and down. Then he starts twisting and turning above the parcel.

Georges: We can see what the little bastard is driving at. So that's why he had come back to see me. I'm such a
scatterbrain: I thought he wanted to take care of my transcendence! But why do they all make such a fuss about the bloody grinding process of the partial object!
Carmen: Georges! My beloved Socrates, I sense that you're hiding something from me. Will you open to me, *psychorama mio*?
Challenger: *Whispering*. Don't do anything! It's probably a trick from the left. I'd rather you gave me the thing—*he points to the parcel with his foot*. Quick! I still have quite a bit of shopping to do: the night is coming and the shops will close. *He goes up and down impatiently*.
Georges: *Stubbornly refusing*. There is no reason to do this! There is no reason to do this! It could only upset me!
Challenger: Cut the crap: if you're a French patriot, you have to give it to the American scholars.
Georges: By Jove! And in no time they'll be coming up with some devilish object!

Challenger is gesticulating like a madman while ordering him to remain silent.

Georges: After Star Wars, the logo war! That's where one hundred years of Lacanism took us! But as far as I know, the Saussurian Conventions of Geneva haven't ruled out the use of signifying gases have they?

Challenger, in one final effort, manages to grasp the parcel with his feet and starts to rise.

Georges: Stop! Not so fast! Sign a receipt or, at least, an acquittal, and I'll go and join him on the road of sex, join him in the alembic of sex!

Georges holds on to Challenger's leg; they both disappear through the ceiling while Carmen keeps on whining, desperately banging on the door.

© Bruno, Emmanuelle, Stephen Guattari, Fonds Guattari, IMEC.

CONTRIBUTORS

Iloe Ariss is a Ph.D. student in the Department of Germanic Languages at Columbia University, New York City, USA.

Benjamin Bandosz is an independent scholar working in Toronto, Canada.

Mikhail Fedorchenko is a Ph.D. student in the Stasis Center for Practical Philosophy at the European University at St Petersburg, Russia.

Flore Garcin-Marrou is Lecturer in Performance and Theatre Studies at the University of Toulouse-Jean Jaurès, France.

Gary Genosko is Professor of Communication Studies at Ontario Tech University, Toronto, Canada.

Jay Hetrick is Associate Professor in Fine Arts at University of Sharjah, U.A.E.

Mahoro Murasawa is Professor of Sociology at Ryukoku University, Kyoto, Japan.

Stéphane Nadaud is a psychiatrist, practicing in Paris, France.

Solène Nicolas is an independent scholar working in Paris, France.

Carlos A. Segovia is an independent philosopher working in Berlin, Germany.

INDEX

absence (*see* lack)
abstract machines 121
Academicism 100, 103
Adrien, Philippe xv, 137
Alcibiade 163
Ananke 92 n.19
Antonioli, Manola 92 n.15
Antonioni, Michelangelo 73
Aperghis, Georges 137
Archimedes 163
Argonauts 104
Aristophanes 74, 92 n.24
Aristotle x, xvii n.14, 68, 115, 140, 142
Artaud, Antonin 119, 120
a-signifying 127
assemblage 108
assemblage (*Ansammlung*) 108
assemblage (*Versammlung*) 108
assembly 100
ATEM 137
autonomist left 137
Autopoiesis 127

Badiou, Alain xi, xviii n.17, 65, 66, 67, 70, 76 n.4, 76 n.5, 76 n.11
Bains, Paul xx n.23
Barthes, Roland 72
Beat Generation 139
Beck, Julian 136
Beckett, Samuel 120, 134, 139, 140, 141, 145
becoming viii, 73, 74, 103
becoming animal 96, 97
being viii, ix, x, xiv, xvi n.7, xvii n.7, xvii n.13, xvii n.14, xix n.22, xx n.22, 71, 73, 79, 80, 81, 84, 85, 86, 88, 89, 90 n.3, 91 n.10, 103, 110, 115, 122, 124, 126
Bellour, Raymond 91 n.15
Bergson, Henri 99
Berressem, Hanjo ix, xvii n.11, 92 n.15
Besse, Jacques 136
Betti, Laura 137
biology 124
black holes 120
Blanchot, Maurice xix n.22
body 123, 124
body art 139
body without organs ix, 96, 120
Boyer, Amalia 76 n.13
Breuer, Josef 72
Brownian dispersion xviii n.21
butoh 96, 97, 98

Caligula 153
capitalism 102
cartographic ontology xvi n.7
catachresis 28, 68, 81
Centrone, Bruno 90 n.4
CERFI 136
chaos xvi, xviii n.21
chaosmic abolition xvi n.7
chaosmic ontology viii
chaosmosis viii
Chernikhov, Yakov 104
Christ Pantocrator 139
clinamen 140
Clover and the bee xx n.22
Cold War 136

INDEX 169

Collett, Guillaume 91 n.9
color(s) in painting 100, 101
comic xv
connection xvii n.13
consistency (*see also* plane of consistency) xviii n.21, 85
Constellations of the universes 96, 99
constructivism (*see also* Russian Constructivism) 96, 103
contradiction 28, 69
Cormann, Enzo xv, 134, 138
Cornelius, Johannes Wilhelm 122
cosmic xv, 72
cyberpunk 124

dada 74, 134
Debussy, Claude 120
Delacroix, Eugène 100
Deleuze, Gilles xi, xiv, xvi n.7, xvii n.7, xviii n.22, xix n.22, 66, 67, 82, 83, 84, 90 n.2, 90 n.7, 91 n.9, 91 n.10, 91 n.15, 92 n.15, 99, 102, 142, 144, 146 n.12
Deligny, Fernand 135
delirium (*see* nonsense)
Delphi 75
desire 69, 82, 88, 89
desiring-machines 84
determinability xviii n.21
dialectics xv
difference (*see also* Many) xviii n.22, xix n.22, 67, 91 n.10
Dike 69, 92 n.19
disclosure 69, 87
discursive 98
disjunction xvii n.13
disjunctive synthesis xviii n.22
disruptions (in narrative, performance, etc.) 71, 122, 125, 127, 141
Dosse, François 124, 128 n.13
Doyle, Arthur Conan x

dramaturgy 120, 122, 125, 126, 127, 134, 135, 136, 137, 138, 139, 140, 141, 142, 143, 144, 145
dualism(s) 69, 72
Dubillard, Roland 136
dynamic disequilibrium 87

early Greek philosophy xvi n.1
earth 114
Eco, Umberto 139
Eleatism 68, 81
enunciation ix, xvii n.13, xviii n.21, 126
Epicurus 140
Eros 69
essences xix n.22
eternal return 126
event 140
existential territories 97, 99

faciality 120
Falsehood 104
Faulkner, William 120
feminine 69, 72, 73
FGERI 136
FHAR 137
figure-signs 84, 86
film (*see also* Minor cinema) xv, 124
flows xvii n.13
Ford Coppola, Francis 125
form in painting 102
Foucault, Michel 120
four functors (*see* ontological functors)
Fourfold (*Geviert*) 114
fractalization ix
French Revolution 100
Freud, Sigmund 72, 75, 120
fundamental ontology viii

German Expressionism 101, 102
Gerould, Daniel 122, 128 n.7, 128 n.8

Ginsberg, Allen 139
Glass, Philip 137
God 91 n.13, 103
Goddard, Michael 121, 128 n.4, 128 n.5, 129 n.21
gods 114
goddess (*see also* Juno) xv, 69, 75, 87, 116, 117, 126
goddesses 69, 92 n.19

heaven 114
Heidegger viii, ix, xiii, xvi n.7, xvii n.7, xvii n.10, 69, 76 n.9, 108, 112, 113, 114, 115, 116, 117 n.2, 118 n.15, 118 n.18, 118 n.25, 126, 129 n.20
henology (*see also* One) xix n.22, 79
Hera (*see* Juno)
Heraclitus viii, xi, xviii n.22, 88
history of painting 100, 101, 102, 103
history of philosophy vii
Hubaut, Joël 138
Huelsenbeck, Richard 74, 77 n.19
humor xv, 65, 105 n.6, 116
Husserl, Edmund 122, 123
Hybris 92 n.19

idea xix n.22, 81, 82, 102, 103, 142, 143
image in painting 100
immanence viii, 66, 123
immaterial universes (*see* constellations of the universes *and* universes of reference or value)
impotence 69
industrial art 102
Ingarden, Roman 122
Institutional psychotherapy 99, 135
institutions 99, 100, 102, 135
Irigaray, Luce 69, 73, 76 n.10

Joyce, James 120
Juno 29, 68, 71, 87, 104, 115, 117, 126
Justice (*see also* Dike) 69

Kafka, Franz x, xv, 120
Kandinsky, Wassily 101, 102
Kant, Immanuel 100, 102, 103, 108, 112, 113
Klein, Melanie 105 n.6
Kramer, Robert 124

La Borde 125, 135, 136
Lacan, Jacques x, xi, xviii n.17, xviii n.21, 82, 87, 90 n.5, 106 n.6, 120, 136, 139, 165
lack 88, 91 n.9
language x, 68, 124
larval subjects 144
Léaud, Jean-Pierre 137
Lebel, Jean-Jacques 136, 138
Leclaire, Serge 91 n.9
Leibniz, Gottfried Wilhelm xiii, xvi n.7, 84, 85, 86, 91 n.15, 92 n.15, 140
less 26, 67, 80, 86, 87
Lévi-Strauss, Claude 87, 92 n.18
life forms 127
lineaism 101
line(s) in painting 100, 101, 102, 103
linguistics 123
literature 124
logic 69, 71, 73, 80, 81, 115, 117
logomachy 143
Logos 87
Lombardo, Stanley 73, 77 n.18
Lucretius 140
lunar cycles 75

macro (*see also* molar) 97
madness xi
Maglioni, Silvia 128 n.15

Malick, Terrence 120
Malina, Judith 136
many xii, xiii, xiv, xvi n.7, xviii n.21, xviii n.22, xix n.22, xx n.22, 25, 65, 67, 68, 71, 74, 81, 82, 83, 84, 85, 86, 89, 91 n.9, 103, 110
Marx, Karl 120
masculine 69, 72, 73, 116
materialism 123
mathematics xii
matter in painting 100
May 1968 97, 136
meaning 68, 69, 71
melody 69
menstrual cycles 75
metaphor(s) 140
Michalski, Bohdan 128 n.9
micro (*see also* molecular) 97, 98
mimesis 142
minor cinema 120, 125
minor literature 120
mockery 74
modes of being 127
modulation of consistency xviii n.21
Moira 92 n.19
molecular 96, 97
molecular revolution 97
monadic politics 85
monadology 91 n.14, 92 n.15
monism (*see also* univocism) 71, 73, 74, 85, 123
monist politics 85
more 67, 80, 86, 87
mortals 114
multiplicity (*see* Many)

Nature 91 n.13, 103, 104
nearness 113
nearness (*Nähe*) 113
necessity (*see also* Ananke)
Nietzsche, Friedrich 92 n.24, 142

noema xiii
noesis xiii
nomadism 144
non-being x, 80, 115
non-discursive 127
nonsense 74, 89
nous 87, 90 n.3
Nouveau Cirque 137

object xiv
object (*Gegenstand*) 112
objective 98, 99
Octavian 153
one(ness) x, xi, xii, xiv, xvii n.7, xviii n.21, xviii n.22, xix n.22, 27, 65, 67, 71, 74, 80, 81, 82, 83, 84, 85, 86, 88, 89, 90 n.3, 91 n.9, 103, 104, 106 n.6, 110, 126, 127
ontological difference xvii n.7
ontological functors (F-Φ-U-T) 92 n.19, 97, 98, 99, 103
ontology (*see also* Being) vii, viii, xiii, xvi n.7, xvii n.7, xix n.22, 67, 79, 83, 84, 85, 86, 122, 124, 126, 127
Otherness xvii n.14, 66, 80
Oury, Jean 135, 145 n.4

Pain, François 138
palimpsest 139
paradox 68, 87
paranoia 127
Parmenides viii, ix, x, xi, xii, xiv, xvii n.7, xvii n.10, xvii n.13, 27, 28, 65, 66, 67, 69, 70, 71, 73, 74, 76 n.8, 79, 80, 81, 86, 87, 88, 89, 90 n.3, 103, 104, 107, 109, 111, 115, 116, 126, 127
Pasolini, Pier Paolo 137
Pataphysics xv, 141
patriarchy 73
people 100, 101

perception 123
Petit, Raymond 135
phenomenology xiii
phenomenon 140
Philibert, Nicholas 125
philo-performance 71
Pirandello, Luigi 140
plane of consistency ix, xvii n.13, xix n.22, 83
Plato vii, viii, x, xi, 65, 66, 67, 70, 74, 75, 75 n.1, 75 n.3, 76 n.7, 77 n.21, 77 n.22, 81, 103, 107, 109, 111, 114, 115, 117 n.3, 118 n.9, 118 n.12, 118 n.21
plurality (*see* many)
poetry xii, 70
point-signs xviii n.21, 82, 86, 90 n.8
Polack, Jean-Claude 145 n.3
politics 85, 95, 97, 98, 99, 124, 137, 138
postmedia 125
power-signs 84, 86
pragmatics 124
pre-Socratics vii, xi, xvi n.7, 69
Proust, Marcel 120
psychedelia 73
psychiatry 98, 99, 135, 136
psychoanalysis 72, 73, 75, 79
psychodrama 88
psychorama 88
psychosomatism 122
Pure form 122

quarks 71
Querrien, Anne xix n.22

Ramnoux, Clémence xviii n.22
real 96
refrains (*see also* Ritornellos) 121, 125, 127, 153, 155
repetition 126

representation xvii n.13, 96, 122, 125, 127
revolution 97, 98, 99, 102, 104, 105
revolutionary machine 96, 97, 98, 99
Rhizomatics x
rhythm(s) 69, 70, 71, 73
ritornellos (*see also* Refrains) 120
Rodchenko, Alexander 101
Romanticism 100, 101
Russian avant-garde 101
Russian Constructivism 96, 100, 101, 102
Russian Revolution 96, 100, 101

Saint-Alban 135
sameness xvii n.14, 66, 80, 88
Santoro, Fernando 73, 77 n.17
Sartre, Jean-Paul 134, 135
Saussure, Ferdinand de 106 n.6, 165
schizoanalysis xiii, 123, 124
Sebeok, Thomas 75
semiotics 124
Severino, Emanuele xix n.22
sexuality 29, 69, 87, 116
shamanism 73
Shannon-Weaver model 75
Signifier 139, 144, 153, 165
Simondon, Gilbert 90 n.1
Sivadon, Danielle 145 n.3
Smith, Daniel 67, 76 n.6
Socrates x, xii, 65, 74, 75, 76, 89, 149, 150, 151, 153, 154, 155, 164
sphere 81
Spielberg, Steven 125
Spinoza, Baruch xvii n.7, xix n.22, 82, 84, 85, 86, 91 n.12, 91 n.13, 99, 103
state 100
statism 100
Sternberg, Jacques 136
Structuralism 140

subject (*see also* larval subjects) xiv, 126, 140
subjective 98, 99, 102
subjectivity xiii, xvi, 72, 97, 98, 99, 102, 124
substance xix n.22, 82, 83, 85, 103, 104, 123

Tanaka, Min xiii, 96, 97, 98
television xv
theater (*see* dramaturgy)
theater of ideas xiii
theater-machine of revolution 96, 98, 99
Themis 69
theory of forms 65
theory of theater (*see* dramaturgy)
therapeutics 98, 135
Thierrée, Jean-Baptiste 133, 136, 137
thing 107, 108, 109, 110, 111, 126
thing (*chose*) 107, 109
thing (*Ding*) 108, 109, 110, 112, 113, 114, 115
thing (*Sache*) 108, 109, 110
thing (*truc*) 27, 28, 71, 107, 113
Thomson, Graeme 128 n.15
time viii, ix, xi, 73
topology 83, 85
Tosquelles, François 135
transcendental subject xiv
transversality 125
trick (*truc*) 79, 86, 87, 89
truth 69, 87

unary time viii, ix, xi
unconcealedness (*see also* disclosure)
unconscious 72, 91 n.9, 92 n.15, 123, 139
unity (*see* one, unary time, univocism)
unity of opposites xviii n.22
universes of reference or value (*see also* constellations of the universes) 97, 99
univocism xi, xvi n.7, xvii n.7, xix n.22, 83, 84, 91 n.10
Uno, Kuniichi xvi n.7

void 126
Voilquin, Jean viii, xvii n.8

Watson, Janell 91 n.15, 128 n.11
Whitehead, Alfred North 91 n.15
Wilson, Bob 137
winter years 137
Witkiewicz, Stanisław Ignacy xiii, 119, 120, 121, 122, 123, 124, 126, 127, 128 n.6, 128 n.18, 128 n.19
woman-mother 126

Yahweh 163
Young, Eugene B. 91 n.15, 128 n.12

Zen Buddhism 104
Zeno of Elea xi, 65, 68, 109